STAGE DESIGN
THROUGHOUT THE WORLD
1970-75

RENÉ HAINAUX

STAGE DESIGN
THROUGHOUT THE WORLD
1970-75

GEORGE G. HARRAP & CO. LTD
LONDON

First published in Belgium 1976
by Editions Meddens S.A., Brussels
First published in Great Britain 1976
by GEORGE G. HARRAP & CO. LTD
182-184 High Holborn, London WC1V 7AX

© *Editions Meddens S.A., Brussels* 1976
English translation © *Editions Meddens S.A., Brussels* 1976

ISBN O 245 52946 2

Printed in Belgium

FOREWORD

Putting this book together has given us great pleasure. Nothing is more agreeable than to rescue from the recesses of the mind the still-fresh memory of a great evening in the theatre – those evenings which, while filling us amply, reawaken our appetites as well.

Many times during the last five years I have felt this sensation : when discovering, to my total surprise, in a London suburb, *Bremer Freiheit* by the young Rainer Werner Fassbinder played by the Hampstead Theatre Club; or when savouring the expected quality of Shakespeare's *Timon*, directed in Paris by Peter Brook.

Naturally enough, this panorama of the great theatrical moments of 1970-1975 would be hopelessy incomplete if it were only a mosaic of my own experiences. Happily, Mr. Ossia Trilling, Vice-President of the International Association of Theatre Critics, helped considerably by agreeing to make up a list of nearly 100 "outstanding" productions. We submitted this list to some 40 correspondents, as well as to the various National Centres of the International Theatre Institute, who sent us the required documentation as well as valuable additions.

*

Most of our readers are aware of the works published earlier by Harrap – Theatre Arts Books – Meddens under our editorship and with the support of the International Theatre Institute :
1. *Stage Design Throughout the World since 1935*. London, Harrap; New York, Theatre Arts Books, 1956.
2. *Stage Design Throughout the World since 1950*. London, Harrap; New York, Theatre Arts Books, 1964.
3. *Stage Design Throughout the World since 1960*. London, Harrap; New York, Theatre Arts Books, 1973.*
The present work is an intermediary volume which will centre on "stage productions" rather than merely on "stage design".

Such a project interested the publishers and, although certain of the ITI Centres had to drop out for lack of financial means, we set to work.

The result : 421 illustrations for 179 productions in 27 countries (some serious lacunae : Latin America is hardly represented, Asia is reduced to merely Japan).

All the productions are presented in chronological order by author, from Aeschylus to the young 27-year-old composer, Andrew Lloyd Webber. This classification allows direct comparisons between, for example, different productions of the same text (*Measure for Measure, Lear, The Wild Duck* or *Liebelei*). It also reveals some curious relationships – their birthdates place Gorki and Rostand side by side! Still, this kind of surprise doesn't hinder generating lines from forming.

Our intention is not to create a prize-list or ranking. Many remarkable plays, and productions of exceptional interest, are not even included. We have not necessarily drawn on just the best works of the last five years, but, more modestly, on the *most discussed* works.

---

* Under the title "Le Décor de Théâtre dans le Monde..." these three works were (like this one) published in French by les Editions Meddens, Bruxelles.

Certain productions are more fully illustrated than others. This is because, for one reason or another, they *seem* more important, or because only an ample iconography can communicate an idea of what they were like.

Our choices will not please everyone. They follow in the line of our earlier work, *Stage Design Throughout the World since 1960;* that is : precedence is given to "non-traditional" productions. Not all novelties or innovations are worth following of course, and many traditional productions retain their charm – but what is the use of describing them ?

As soon as the shores of the "non-traditional" are reached, the compass begins to spin. We become disoriented and the concept of genres loses its clarity.

So much so, that in the last five years, breaks with the tradition have multiplied : received ideas and accepted forms are equally rejected.

In his *Mise en crise théâtrale,* Emile Copfermann declares : "The disappearance of the myth of "culture" allows the birth of an occasional theatre, non-repetitive, non-transportable and non-normative, a theatre of auto-consumption, of transgression, which wants to and must pose new problems for itself."

The idea that the theatre is dying is less popular today, at the same time as the cries grow louder of those who demand its condemnation. Thus there is reason enough to be optimistic. We are living through a period of intense experiment and violent change. Personally, I believe that this lustre is as exciting, as productive as that of 1920-1925.

René Hainaux

ACKNOWLEDGMENTS

It is to our correspondents and to certain National Centres of the International Theatre Institute that we owe the great amount of material received. We thank the various theatres for the documents which they authorized us to publish, the designers for their models and plans, the photographers for their photos – and also each and every author, director, designer for their letters, interviews and statements, articles, programs or books.

Our correspondents or the ITI centres handled the delicate problem of copyright. Our particular gratitude goes to Mr. Lamberto V. Avellana (Philippine Centre), Mrs. Margareta Barbutza (Rumanian Centre), Mr. Herbert Barth (Bayreuther Festspiele), Miss Yolande Bird and Mr. Walter Lucas (British Centre), Mr. Alain Crombecque (France), Mr. Friedrich Dieckmann (ITI Centre and IOSTT of the German Democratic Republic), Mrs. Gerda Dietrich and Mr. Joachim W. Preuss (ITI Centre of the Federal Republic of Germany), Mrs. Helga Dostal (Austrian Centre), Mrs. Suzanne Gal (Hungarian Centre), Professor Denis Gontard (France), Mrs. Judith Gottlieb and Mr. Jesaja Weinberg (Israeli Centre), Mr. Vassili Goussev (USSR Centre), Mr. Zygmunt Hübner (Polish Centre), Mr. Mark Hermans (Belgian Centre), Messrs. Kaoru Kanamori and Akira Wakabayashi (Japan), Mr. Arvi Kivimaa and Miss Riitta Seppälä (Finnish Centre), Mrs. Ingrid Luterkort (Swedish Centre), the late Robert MacGregor (United States), Mr. Paul-Louis Mignon (French Centre), Mrs. Olga Milanovic (Yugoslavia), Mr. Juozas Miltinis (Lithuania), Mrs. Elena Povoledo and Mr. Vincenzo Torraca (Italy), Mrs. Eva Soukupova (Czech Centre), Professor Edmund Stadler (Switzerland), Mrs. Marlis Thiersch (Australian Centre), and Mr. Max Wagener (Dutch Centre).

As we have mentioned elsewhere, it was Mr Ossia Trilling, Vice-President of the International Association of Theatre Critics, who compiled our first selection of productions.

Mr. Michael Nash, our former student at Cornell, is the author of the English version.

The layout was prepared by M. Frans Van den Bremt, with the help of Mrs. Francine De Boeck.

Lastly the tasks of secretary-documentalist were assumed by Mrs. Nicole Leclercq.

A BIRD'S-EYE VIEW
OF SOME NEW TRENDS

Among other things, the protest movement of 1968 sought to give new power to the creative imagination. This desire was not without its effects and many new doors were opened, particularly in the area of theatrical production.

To be more specific: for those under twenty-five today, the unrest of 1968 belongs to a History through which they never lived. To those who fought in the ranks they offer the respect due to all "veterans" – but without necessarily accepting their ideas. From this has resulted a wave of disengagement.

The protesters of 1968 are thirty today, or even older. Many have dropped out or become tired. Some have returned to the fold. But not all. Curiously enough, it's among the least young, I believe, that 1968 has had the greatest repercussions. Giorgio Strehler touches on these effects:

The idea of a popular theatre was a very beautiful dream. Like all dreams, it had, despite its historical importance, a certain element of illusion. This dream haunted the youth of my generation and, personally, I remained attached to it up until the day I became aware that the historical moment had a certain rhythm and certain characteristics which need to be respected, and that reality, with all its constraints, didn't always correspond to the utopian vision I had constructed. Although this discovery was disconcerting for many among us, we are obliged to admit that in the real world, given a consumer society and mass communications, there can exist only theatre for an elite. I mean simply that the theatre can not reach 10,000 people at once as can a football match... "Elite" is not necessarily synonymous with evening dress...

Our generation fought to the end against "bourgeois" theatre. Yet today we learn that many of the young speak of the work we do as another form of "bourgeois" theatre – thus, to be destroyed...

History has progressed and has shown us continually that different points of view may coexist. It even follows from this lesson that one must experiment with differing methodologies, even opposing ones. Thus, it is not just possible but desirable (for this possibility represents to us a conquest, a truly positive cultural phenomenon) that the Living Theatre and the Berliner Ensemble coexist. For, although they contradict each other, they are parts of the same type of cultural phenomenon. It is likewise good that Peter Brook can present during the same season works as different as *Orghast* and *Midsummer Night's Dream*.

Our recent history allows us great possibilities of theatrical expression, as opposed to the prejudices which once obliged us to hold to a single style. This explosion, this infinite multiplication of possibilities – which, at first glance, may seem a diffusion of effort but, on the contrary, allows us to gain the open spaces – is perhaps the most extraordinary phenomenon of our time.

And Strehler again: "The way to remake the popular theatre is no longer to bring people together, but to divide them; it is no longer to create a celebratory communion, but to force people into a dialectical process."

In Europe, this total and ceaseless questioning is manifested in numerous areas, in education as in sexology, in sociology as in the arts – it is both a fashion and more than a fashion.

With a devastating violence, most of the "young" directors in the theatre refuse identification and reject psychology. When they fail, they do so with soulless spectacles that are intolerably boring. But when they succeed, their productions inspire an unreserved enthusiasm through a combination of originality, acute intelligence and incandescent artistry. It isn't always easy to distinguish between what is merely a return to Meyerhold's "theatrical theatre" and what might be a new victory of the spirit.

A theatre not of being, but of becoming: the spectacle is no longer presented as a solution, but as pure process, a difficult path toward an as yet undefinable truth.

We would like this preface to match the rhythm of the illustrations which follow. It will begin, therefore, with Aeschylus and recent performances of Greek tragedy.

And first of all, with *The Oresteia,* directed by Luca Ronconi (ill. 1-7). Ronconi's vision is rooted in the orientation just described. He declares for example:

As in my preceeding works, in place of a search for a unique voice, I preferred to organize the production around simultaneous, differing interpretations...

I tend to think of *The Oresteia* less as a monolithic block than as a heterogeneous ensemble whose unity will only be visible *a posteriori,* in the mind of the spectator.

In his excellent study (¹), Franco Quadri discusses some of the choices which Ronconi faced:

From the first *stasima* of *Agamemnon,* the murkiest yet also the most fascinating of the tragedies, the themes explored are innumerable; each one could be the point of departure of a new production. The director must choose between the obsession of divine punishment which menaces impious men and the particular malediction which strikes the descendants of Atreus, between the story of the Trojan War and allusions to the Orphic mysteries. Or he could read *The Oresteia* as a series of sea voyage stories, from the Orient to Greece and back, followed by a summary of the tribulations of Orestes...

Or should the double kidnapping of priestesses – Helen at the beginning, and Cassandra at the end, of the Trojan War – be seen as the symbol of a cultural/religious exchange?...

And isn't Cassandra's true role to import to Greece the cult of the oriental god Apollo? Doesn't the conflict which divides the family of Atreus reflect that of two religions disputing the same sphere of influence? Aren't the trials of Orestes, Apollo's protégé, symbols of the difficulties encountered by the new religion as it seeks a foothold?...

Because nothing is certain in Aeschylus' trilogy save its very obscurity, it is on this that Ronconi bases his production. He imagines an *Oresteia* rediscovered in the Middle Ages by a world unaware of the ancient rites and myths apart from certain abstract notions passed on by Aristotle...

Ronconi imagines four distinct historical epochs in the chorus: the first is that of prehistory, source of all myths; the second, that of the Trojan War, anterior to the author. The third belongs to Aeschylus and his public, a public which had experienced the Persian wars and, consequently, was sensitized to any conflict between East and West.

(¹) Franco Quadri: *Il Rito perduto. Luca Ronconi* (Torino, G. Einaudi, 1973).

And the fourth epoch is that of the Middle Ages, a time about equidistant between Aeschylus and us...

What interests him is to discover and specify four mental attitudes vis-à-vis the text, attitudes which can even coexist in a single individual.

Given this reading, the traditional unity of the chorus will be broken, the twelve chorus members will be spread all over the stage, each playing in his own way the text while participating in an action unrelated to his own words.

This approach finds a parallel in the reflections of George Thomson :[1]
The kingdom of the Law has begun. Thinking that we observe the fate of Orestes, we are witnessing in reality the birth and affirmation of Law in society.

Once considered to be an offense that the victim's family must revenge, murder in another historical period appears as a profanation that the guilty one must expiate according to rules established by a powerful sacerdotal caste. Even later, it becomes a crime against society, to be judged by a legally constituted popular tribunal. From this evolution we deduce that the tribal regime was first supplanted by an aristocratic regime, which, in turn, had to give way to democracy, founded on the supremacy of the man over the woman and on an equitable distribution of the common goods.

Finally, Quadri vividly describes the performance. Here is the first episode :
The central door opens again. Behind it appears the palace, a wooden tower with a steep exterior stairway. The palace door opens with a sinister groan and an avalanche of clods of dirt tumbles from step to step to pile up at the bottom. Another mound of earth, a kind of concave barrow, surges up from a trap directly across from the first. Then, announced by these mysterious signs, Clytemnestra (Marisa Fabbri) appears at the palace door, her eyes haggard, hair bristling, with a hard expression, an imperious air. A striking apparition. With jerky steps she moves barefoot down the steps which are now encumbered by dirt. Her very stiff costume is sumptuous and barbarian : a brown woolen cape, woven with gold and encrusted with colored stones about the stomach, covers a coarse white dress, very simply cut. While descending, the Queen begins to speak in a slow voice, a voice both exalting and despairing. She answers with kindness the questions of the Chorus Leader; then, she seems to sink into an intense stupor. Her words fight each other. The sentences are broken up by question marks and suspended pauses. Each time she suddenly stops speaking – that is, with nearly every word – we fear it will be forever. Each pause is an abyss. The bridges are all destroyed, the linking words have been lost or forgotten. Then, suddenly, after having made us feel all the seriousness of this drama, the Queen rediscovers the missing word. She finds it before our eyes, painfully drawing it from the darkness, and finally she offers it, beautiful and new, for our comfort. Unbelievable as it might seem, this suspense is renewed with each speech, leading us to think that the words coming from her mouth had never existed before. Certain expressions acquire in this way an unusual symbolic dimension.

Quadri goes on to place the production in a larger context :
Ronconi's goal is to reinvent a way of communicating with others and with oneself for a period in which all the known means have lost their value. It's not by accident that the contemporary experimental theatre is searching for new formulas, from the twenty-four hour performances of Bob Wilson (when his hallucinatory marathons don't last a week without interruption) to the "water-theatre" of Patrice Chéreau, with a stop at the neo-constructivism of Victor Garcia (who built a circular tower for Genet's The Balcony, complete with elevators and transparent spirals, to replace the proscenium stage of his theatre). Nor is it accidental that directors everywhere are searching to go back to the sources of language : even putting aside Peter Brook, there remains the ceremony in Latin and ancient Greek which was Serban's Medea.

This first production deserved such a long look because we find in it, pushed to extremes, many of the characteristics of the period : a multiplicity of co-existent interpretations, an antipsychological style, the search for a non-traditional theatrical space. There are similar "family" resemblances between productions as otherwise dissimilar as Dionysos

69, by the Performance Group of New York ([1]), and Die Antiken, done by Berlin's Schaubühne.

France produces few Greek tragedies, and so Antoine Vitez' version of Electra (ill. 8-10) is even more striking :
Antoine Vitez plays before about one hundred spectators seated on two facing bleacher units. The actors utilize a long, narrow mat, similar to the one on which fencers compete but painted in red. When not "on stage", they sit as simply as possible, both present and absent at once, at each end of the playing area. Clearly, Vitez sought to give back to the actor his quasi-religious function, to remind him that he is both part of and outside of the action (the agon). The spectator himself becomes conscious in this way of the limitations of theatre and its temporal truth. And it is in this perspective that the poems of Yannis Ritsos were incorporated into Sophocles' tragedy – to remind us of the suffering of today's Greece.

(Guy Dumur, Nouvel Observateur)
And Vitez himself : "All the developments are mounted one next to the other, and the resulting montage of styles leads in general to the dismemberment of style."

Drawing by Yannis Kokkos for Sophocles' Electra directed by Antoine Vitez.

Shakespeare is a world unto himself. Of the outpouring of new productions between 1970 and 1975, we shall retain just four : those of Lioubimov for Hamlet, Steiger (Measure for Measure), Strehler (King Lear), and Brook (Timon of Athens).

Yourij Lioubimov began his Hamlet (ill. 26-30) with a prologue that brought the entire cast on stage. It was then "...that a dark mass advances laterally, sweeping the stage from left to right, and the actors reel and fall, routed by this vague mass which swallows them up. This mysterious curtain (...) is left alone on the empty stage, just as at the end of the show it will remain alone and triumphant, having cleaned the stage of all the corpses littering it." The collaboration of the director and designer David Borovskij is described by Béatrice Picon-Vallin in Travail Théâtral, no. VIII : [2]
The curtain has both practical and symbolic value. Practical because, being mobile in all directions, able to move parallel, perpendicular or obliquely to the footlights, it allows spontaneous improvisation of the scenic space, keeping us fully conscious of being in a theatre.

A wooden bench, later to be used as a coffin, is placed under the curtain and we see the Queen's chamber. With Claudius and Gertrude seated side by side against it, in frozen positions and with sword blades as armrests, the curtain creates a throne room. Set obliquely, it becomes a wall, at the end of which Hamlet sits. And Hamlet and Ophelia turn it into a cradle, giving it a back and forth movement...

[1] George Thomson : Aeschylus and Athens (New York, Grosset and Dunlap, 1968).

[1] See Stage Design throughout the World since 1960 (London : Harrap; New York : Theatre Arts Books 1973) pp. 30-31.
[2] See Travail Théâtral, "Cahiers trimestriels", direction de la rédaction : D. Bablet, E. Copfermann, B. Dort, F. Kourilsky, C. Olivier (Lausanne : Editions l'Age d'Homme). 19 issues between August 1970 and Spring 1975.

Finally, the curtain is also a curtain: the characters enter and exit by raising parts of it up; and it's by arranging the way it hangs that the traveling players end their rehearsals and begin their performance on the bare stage, covered only by a square carpet.

But the curtain is also more than just a mobile element used in an organic way... Made with a thick workmanship one might call crochet – an irregular lace of coarse wool half-way between gray and brown, whose other side has an unfinished texture, threads hanging in evil bunches accentuating the impression of savage, raw material – the curtain allows infinite lighting effects which all multiply and repeat the central image: that of a prison.

André Steiger trusted Claude Lemaire with the images of *Measure for Measure* (ill. 31-35). In front of a white, shining plastic curtain, Lemaire placed an out of proportion table: the "table of power", the table where decisions are made, the table, too, which will turn into a prison, or a cat-walk for the marionette handler.

The production's program specifically discussed its intentions. We shall reproduce here some of its aphorisms:

To make a spectacle is first of all to take great liberties with a text and an author, and to do so in such a way that the audience shares in this freedom. In so far as the theatre involves History, it can choose among three options: to deny History, to control History, or to un-mask History. The boulevard theatre, for example, denies it, propagandist theatre controls it, and the educational-informative theatre must, always, un-mask it.

The traditional – that is, naturalistic – theatre, in which the actors try to give their characters the appearance of everyday reality, shields the events it represents from the critical sense of the spectator, by making them unfold "as if controlled by some natural law" of psychology...

Assumptions of the first readings:

Psychological behaviours (deviances/disturbances/conflicts) and the justifications given for them by the "powerful", MASK the manipulations used by them in the exercise of POWER.

but, IN RETURN:

their social behaviours reflect the fact that they are "manipulated" by an ideological system they do not control (although they are the privileged instruments of its domination).

THUS: the production must reveal the MASQUERADE (the mask) and the FARCE... The actors must show us the DISTORTION which exists between the words and actions of the characters...

We must present something to be seen, deciphered, "read", INTERPRETED, and do so in such a way that the elements of our theatrical "play" may be used by the public toward ends not necessarily identical with our own.

In doing *King Lear* (ill. 42-45), Giorgio Strehler didn't wish to choose among the allegorical, political and metaphysical fables of the play.

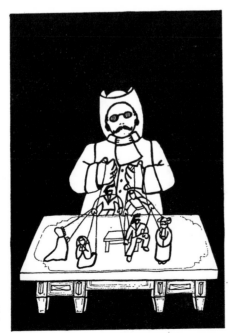

Poster by Francine De Boeck for *Measure for Measure* directed by André Steiger.

Instead, he succeeds in imposing his global vision: "...a great theatre of fools, a huge "circus-world", a cosmic arena for the representation of life and history."

The performance unfolds inside a circular drop stretched and held by ropes, a truncated big-top which defines an arena: a strange material, blackish, shiny gravel which hasn't the weight nor the density of stone, recalls in its lightness the sawdust spread over the circus floor. (¹)

In his preface to *Les Lieux du Spectacle* (²), Peter Brook writes:

For several years, the theatre has been advancing again and, what a coincidence, not in traditional spaces. Have we examined thoroughly enough the reasons for this?

In its time, the structure of the bourgeois theatre corresponded adequately to its function. But, unhappily, those buildings have lasted longer than today's cars, supermarkets and houses. The theatre, therefore, is burdened with a useless heritage.

In choosing to mount *Timon of Athens* (ill. 57-63) in a fundamentally reconstructed Théâtre des Bouffes du Nord, Brook was faithful to this belief.

Christian Crahay, one of his actors, describes the changes made in a letter to us:

The house – ground floor. The seats of the orchestra have dissapeared. In place of the inclined plane up to the orchestra pit which supported these seats, there is a horizontal concrete slab. The orchestra pit remains, covered by a removable wooden unit: the pit itself will be Timon's cave. The old orchestra's central space is used as the main playing area; the ring of space under the balconies is covered with raked platforms holding wooden benches for the audience.

The theatre's original condition remains unaltered. Painted stucco mouldings still cover the wooden balconies, and the ruined or fallen sections have neither been replaced nor restored. Traces of the old paint are visible: red, ochre, green... The flooring of the various stories is new, but the boards are bare, neither painted or covered.

The stage – playing area. The old orchestra is now the main playing area. The raised stage behind the great proscenium arch has given way to a pit six meters deep. Stairways and a landing have been built so this pit might serve as a playing area at various levels. Four doors have been cut in the uprights of the old proscenium arch, revealing the influence of the Elizabethan theatre: one in each wall of the ground floor, one at 1st balcony level stage right, a fourth at 2nd balcony level stage left.

Let us leave Shakespeare for Marlowe. *The Massacre at Paris* (ill. 64-69) or "the sewers of history": the subtitle explains, a bit summarily of course, Richard Peduzzi's design. "The safety curtain opens and closes on a blind wall of weathered bricks which follows a riverbank path stage right. Stage left are two tall buildings with opaque stained glass. In the middle, an area of water, perhaps 25 centimeters deep. There, the conspirators flounder and the dead swim."

(Jean-Pierre Léonardini, *Travail Théâtral*, no. VIII).

We must involve ourselves with details to appreciate the ingenuity of the design conceived by Arie Navon for *Doctor Faustus* (ill. 70). The set built in the form of an hour-glass, is meant to symbolize Faustus' race against time. The two halves of the hour-glass are transparent, built of wire netting stretched over a skeleton of iron poles and constituting a design of broken glass. The upper half is suspended from above and the lower one rests on a revolving stage so that it may be turned toward the audience with either its concave or convex sides. Its convex side becomes Faustus' study; the concave side shelters various scenes, notably those of purgatory. The entire structure is enveloped by a two-story scaffolding: at 3.80 meters there is a verandah for the Angel and her attendants, and at 2.80 meters another verandah for the devils, with a shoot allowing the actors to slide to the floor. Behind the upper half of the hour glass is suspended a small walkway upon which Faustus

(¹) To appreciate the diversity of intentions of this *Lear,* see Giorgio Strehler, *Il Re Lear di Shakespeare* (Verona: Bertani, 1973). The appearance of entire works devoted to one production is another new aspect of the period from 1970-1975.

(²) *Les Lieux du Spectacle – Osaka 70.* Issue conceived and edited by Christian Dupavillon. *L'Architecture d'Aujourd'hui.* No. 152, October-November 1970.

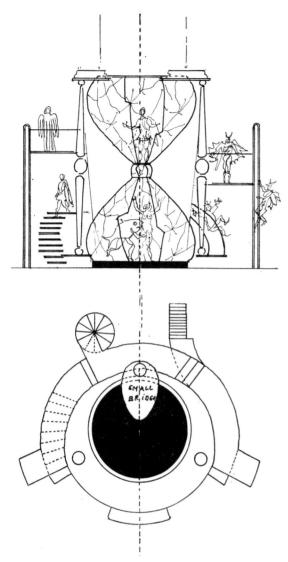

The setting by Arie Navon for *Dr. Faustus.*

appears during his flight. To all this are added cloud projections, lighting effects, etc.

A bit more than ten years ago, Roger Planchon mounted *Tartuffe* in an astonishing setting by René Allio ([1]). In that production he suggested the possibility of Orgon having homosexual penchants. Today he presents a totally different version with an equally astonishing scenography by Hubert Monloup and with Jacques Schmidt's intentionally slovenly costumes (ill. 71-78). Many questions have been raised concerning the relations between the meanings given to Molière's text and its visual presentation. But for me, at least, those relations are, at the same time, very simple, marvelously complex and rigorously faithful to Molière. The production had to take into account Molière's bourgeois realism and, thus, the direction of the actors was based on realistic psychology (in which all actions are based on detectable motivations). But it was also necessary to combine this realism with Molièresque madness : the bewilderment of the characters, the buoyant folly of the intrigues. And nothing could add this dimension better than a violently baroque design, this kind of palace in the midst of redecorating in which Planchon moves his characters.

In his *Candide* (ill. 94-96) Roberto Guicciardini hardly respects Voltaire to the letter : "This stage version", he writes, "is not merely a transposition of Voltaire's novel to the theatre. Diverse material is borrowed from contemporary literature : such borrowings shed light on the contradictions in and contribute to the critical efficacy of the fable."

([1]) See *Stage Design throughout the World since 1950* (London : Harrap ; New York : Theatre Arts Books, 1964) p. 84.

With *The Mistress of the Inn* (ill. 99-100) it is also to a critical vision that Mario Missiroli aspires :

It seems to me reasonable to recognize something more in Goldoni beyond his image as a *galant homme* and the pleasantness of his creations; to render a bit of the particular stain, the horrible hygienic and sanitary state of affairs, the unbridled filth, the brilliant and ambiguous rationality, the disquieting delicacy and furious capitalist misery...

It suffices to decide that the "play" of Mirandolina is no "play", but the simple truth – then everything explains itself : the inn as a microcosm of society, the guests as the declining class, Fabrizio as a starveling in rags, the buffoons as images of the freedom of the irrational, the chevalier as an image of the new sickness of modern times, and Mirandolina herself – sex, placenta and boutique – very exactly the boutique owner of a society of boutiques.

We can not hope in a few lines to describe the recent tendencies of the musical theatre.

Nonetheless, we must point out that the efforts of Walter Felsenstein to give new life to the acting of singers have had repercussions everywhere. The pure beauties of song still have admirers, but more and more the public appreciates quality acting as well. Moreover, the idea of a "critical" opera has taken hold, and indignation sparked by the "social criticism" of a Götz Friedrich has not kept this Eastern European director from being engaged by many major Opera Houses.

Mozart, Wagner and Verdi continue to furnish pretexts for brilliant scenographic experiments.

According to Jacques Lonchampt *(Le Monde),* Giorgio Strehler and Luciano Damiani made brilliant use of Salzburg's Grosses Festspielhaus for *The Magic Flute* (ill. 106-112) :

Strehler and Damiani created a nearly perfect setting, faithful to the naïvete as well as to the philosophical horizon of this enchanting opera. A pleated, yellow curtain is lit by two angled rays of light, suggesting the masonic symbol. It opens on a vast bare space, shining like an icy surface, desert-like and esoteric, limited in the distance by a drop, the symbol of the celestial dome. The drop is raised occassionaly to form triangular openings which let certain elements of the setting pass, or the choruses, messengers carrying the secrets of the universe. The kingdom of night and the starry sky itself exist inside this tent, as if to say that they don't contain the last word of the world, but belong instead to a lesser domain, "to the earth" – from where emerge an amusing temple of Women, the rocks, clouds and cardboard moon of the Queen of Night, dominated by a huge bat's wing. (...) The palm trees, pyramids and grottos appear and disappear like mirages, showing that everything is an illusion, save the wisdom which alone must be pursued.

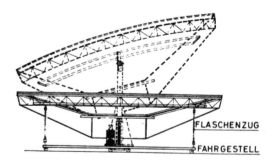

VORDERANSICHT

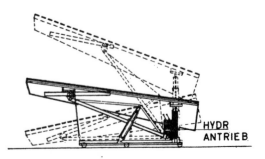

Segments of the revolving stage for *The Ring.*

SEITENANSICHT

The temple of Wagner, Bayreuth, has lost none of its great post-War acquisitions, the years when Wieland Wagner was thought of as an iconoclast by the traditionalists. His brother Wolfgang has taken up the torch, and his production of *The Ring* (ill. 131-139) is a gigantic undertaking whose coherence is assured by both a unity of direction – Wolfgang Wagner directed and designed – and the invention of a revolving stage divided into unequal segments which is used throughout the Tetralogy. By itself this revolve deserves a detailed technical description. The photographs and drawings we are publishing here give only a feeble image of the extraordinary possibilites of this unique design.

In Maurice Béjart's production of *La Traviata* (ill. 140-142) we discover again the "theatre in the theatre". What Béjart gives us is not a story, that of Violetta, alias the Dame aux Camélias, but a performance, that of a famous opera called *Traviata*. In fact, the curtain opens to reveal a reconstruction of a proscenium auditorium which is none other than that of the Monnaie: the house is reflected on the stage, the spectators see themselves in the extras who people the set. And this doubling is extended even to include certain characters. "The opera is not meant to tell us a story", says Béjart, "but to make us dream a story".

The frontiers of the musical theatre occasionally become vague. Certainly, an entire group of contemporary composers – artists recognized as such – continues to produce operas: thus, Paul Dessau, at 80, creates his *Einstein* (ill. 225-227).
And musical comedy remains recognizable as a genre even when it turns to "pop" or "rock", as it did with *Jesus Christ Superstar* (ill. 409-421), very coldly received by critics but a great popular success.
But how should a production like *Kyldex* (ill. 308-312) be classified? As musical theatre undoubtedly, given the concrete music of Pierre Henry. But the kinetic images of Nicolas Schöffer and the important choreography by Alwin Nikolais call out perhaps for the broader appellation of "total theatre". And don't the efforts of Kagel, Cage, Ligeti, Pousseur, Berio or Penderecki often present similar classification problems?

This brief incursion into the musical theatre has drawn us from our chronology. Let us move on to the 19th Century.
Ibsen's *Peer Gynt* (ill. 163-168), created by Berlin's Schaubühne, is incontestably one of the beacon productions of the last five years. The director, Peter Stein, sees Ibsen's text as a document allowing us a critical understanding of the 19th century's *petite bourgeoisie*. He sought to rediscover the sense of fantasy particular to that period and, for this, the collective which is the Schaubühne immersed itself in popular iconography, etchings and comic-strips of the period. The result is multicolored and Peer is revealed as the opposite of a hero. The play is performed over two evenings and the role of Peer is shared among six actors. Two of them play moments of the role which are far apart temporally: Bruno Grenz, for example, plays not only the young Peer seduced by the Trolls, but also the old Peer who returns to his homeland. The actor doesn't renounce identification, yet remains conscious that he's *showing*.

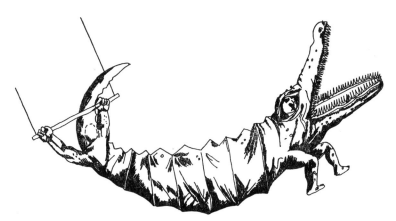

The crocodile in *Einstein*. Drawing by Andreas Reinhardt.

"In *Peer Gynt*", says Peter Stein, "we tried to combine different kinds of space: at each side the two small stages and between them the large area for Peer's travels, at once real and imaginary. For us, it was also important that the audience, seated on two galleries running the length of this structure, be physically close to Peer's tribulations. This need for the proximity of the spectator is found in much of our work."
Bernard Dort interviewed Stein for *Travail Théâtral* (no. IX): "It's been said that, with *Peer Gynt,* you returned to a theatre of illusion. Max Reinhardt has been cited in regards to your work." Stein answered:
> Pure rubbish. *Peer Gynt* has nothing to do with all that. Don't forget that the horses in the play are totally false – stuffed horses. In Reinhardt's theatre they would have been living horses. The difference is not trivial. Their sole authority derives from being truly stuffed. Like the cat on the table – also stuffed. Everything which is used – let's say, rather, cited – creates to a certain extent an illusion, but almost casually. Besides, all these objects and properties have their own role to play in *Peer Gynt*. They become like a museum – the museum which is in the mind of Peer Gynt and that Ibsen already describes to us as such. We have underlined it, willingly and polemically: all that Peer Gynt says, does or thinks, all that a *petit-bourgeois* gifted with a bit of imagination can say, or do, or think, all that, has already been said, done or thought a hundred times, a hundred thousand times; and we have to approach them as we do paintings, objects and mummies which are displayed in the museums. They are all second-hand things and experiences, with which nothing purely personal can be done. To show this became an integral part of the production. *Peer Gynt* describes an illusion. So I find it comical that I'm accused of returning to the theatre of illusion.

And farther on Stein says: "The pseudo-richness of *Peer Gynt* is itself the object of the story Ibsen tells us. Few people have understood this.
We wanted to bring on the stage all the objects, all the images which come back to us from our childhood, from the magic lanterns, etc."

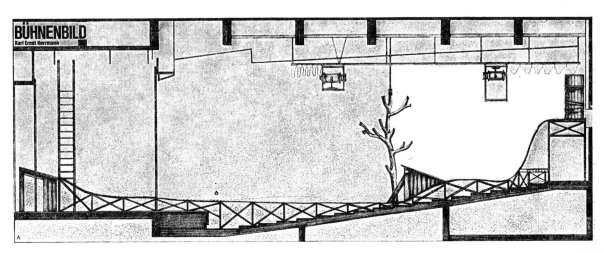

Peer Gynt at the Schaubühne.

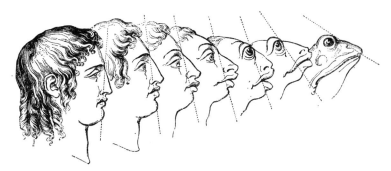

Peer Gynt at the Schaubühne.

It's impossible to leave this production without saying something about the company itself. Founded in 1970, the Neue Schaubühne am Halleschen Ufer seeks to be a model of co-direction based on the collective responsibility of all. It is one of a few recently created companies throughout the world which have profoundly modified the theatrical panorama. Each of its productions has stimulated lively interest with the public and critics. In the present work we have included its *The Pot* (ill. 143-144) as well as its *Stories from the Viennese Wood* (ill. 256-257). Due to our limited space, but against our wishes, we had to do without its *Optimistic Tragedy* (Vichnevski), *Prince of Homburg* (Kleist) and its two-evening production on ancient tragedy.

As during any flourishing period, 1970-1975 saw a modification in theatrical centers of interest.

True, most of the major theatres remained productive: the Bolshoi in Moscow, La Scala in Milan, Berlin's Schiller Theatre, the National Theatre of London. But in what could be called the experimental theatre, the leading roles went to newcomers: La Mama attracted less attention (although Ellen Stewart developed and expanded her activity) than Robert Wilson and his Byrd Hoffman School; Jozef Szajna took the lead over Jerzy Grotowski, even though Grotowski's *Apocalypsis cum figuris* is one of the most important productions of the last few years. The Living Theatre split up while, in Prague, the Za Branou disappeared, a victim of repression.

New companies attracted great interest: Berlin's Schaubühne, which we have just discussed, the Nuria Espert company (ill. 248-249), the Grand Magic Circus (ill. 374-375 and 397-404), the James Joyce Liquid Memorial Theatre, the Nouvelle Scène Internationale... And others, only slightly older, come to the fore: the Théâtre du Soleil (ill. 379-390), the Odin Teatret (ill. 155-162)...

It is not our intention to compose a prize-list. But we must point out that, along with these newcomers, certain long-established directors and theatres have not renounced the search for new ways, and that their courage has often been rewarded with success: the Compagnie Madeleine Renaud – Jean-Louis Barrault, Tovstonogov and his Gorki Theatre like Lioubimov and his Taganka (ill. 26-30), Benno Besson working presently at the Volksbühne (ill. 241-242, 297, 319-323)... Joseph Papp extends his empire systematically from its center in the New York Shakespeare Festival, the Royal Court tirelessly continues its search for new plays and authors, and Dario Fo constantly adapts his work to local political circumstances.

This incomplete enumeration indicates sufficiently that, during the last few years, the theatre has been in flux – the theatre still lives.

Again let us return to our chronology. Passing over Strindberg and Chekhov (perenially popular authors), we note a renewed interest, and not just in German-speaking countries, in Schnitzler, Wedekind and Sternheim. Then we come to Brecht.

The vogue of Brecht has grown constantly since his death – so much so that some countries discover, after a given season, that he was played more often than Shakespeare!

Brecht's successors at the Berliner Ensemble have always insisted that truly following his example means pushing his techniques farther ahead, constantly renewing the way his works are produced. It was fidelity seen in this perspective that led Giorgio Strehler to present a second version of *Threepenny Opera* (ill. 231-232) when his first production had so satisfied Brecht himself. Strehler's preoccupations were numerous and he analyzes them clearly in the following passage:

The central problem in directing *Threepenny Opera* is that it "appears to be" edible, while all the while "being" inedible: the appearance of *divertissement* which becomes progressively alarming; an "agreable" evasion which becomes disagreeable and even directly (or indirectly) aggressive. It would be just as mistaken to present *Threepenny* as a vision of some colorful proletarian underworld, full of fantasy and even "aggressively" inoffensive, as it would be to do it as an unequivocal, sinister, brutal "act" of violence which terrifies a bourgeois public. The one tends to exclude the other, and this "against" the text, against its wish to be, in its way, within certain limits, "ambiguous". Within the limits, to be more specific, of one of the five manners of telling the truth when one can't. Ambiguous, but voluntarily so, out of methodological choice, not ideological incapacity or insufficiency.

Consequently, *Threepenny Opera* "plays" the play of bourgeois society from the inside, with some of the weapons proper to that society alone (from the picturesque to the pathetic, from the generic revolutionary to the song). Few productions of *Threepenny* to this day have managed to bring this off – the Pabst film less than any other.

Benno Besson too rethought, after several years, his interpretation of *The Good Woman of Setzuan* (ill. 241-242). The most recent version categorically turns its back on *chinoiserie*, but also escapes the trap of realistic modernization, notably through masks made out of deforming elements covered by stockings.

With his *Mother Courage* (ill. 240), Antoine Vitez ventured even farther: "It is not a production in the epic style", he tells us. But Vitez adds: "...Brecht ought to be treated with disrespect; nothing could be more Brechtian, right?"

The stage represents a road, the road that Courage travels perpetually with her wagon – to be specific, a baby carriage. On the platforms which border the road is piled the debris of our own age: detergent boxes, plastic bottles, old tires, etc. Vitez de-codes Brecht for us. What Brecht wanted to write about, according to the director, was not the Thirty Years War, but the war of 1914-1918. Thus the costumes and properties suggest no particular period. And finally, Vitez wants to create a non-figurative theatre. If he doesn't go so far as to give us a "collage" of texts, he allows himself a "collage" of images. In short: an unorthodox production which wants to be thought of as faithful – in its own way.

Brecht's earlier works have recently been the beneficiaries of revivals by the younger companies (particularly *The Wedding of the Petits-Bourgeois*). Their expressionist resonances are now accepted with much less apprehension than before.

For its part, the Berliner Ensemble continues to break new Brecht ground. After having exhumed *The Breadshop* it presented *Turandot* (ill. 243-247).

Beginning with Eduardo De Filippo, born in 1900 (ill. 252-253), we come to the motley cohort of 20th Century authors.

Our decision to organize the productions of 1970-1975 in chronological order by author has curious consequences, some of which may appear annoying. It becomes impossible, for example, to group authors by artistic schools, by political ideologies, or, more simply, by nationalities. On the other hand, our organization opens other perspectives.

Let us establish a first group consisting of those authors born more than fifty years ago (ie. before 1925). We note immediately that certain playwrights already dead or long forgotten, such as Ödön von Horvath or Marieluise Fleisser, have returned curiously into fashion (ill. 256-257 and 254-255): von Horvath for his denunciation of Viennese sentimentality, and Fleisser because her work prefigures contemporary German dramaturgy. Others continue to write plays and their efforts are produced often – Anouilh, Dürrenmatt, Frisch, Miller, Williams – but their recent plays add little to their reputations. Others still no longer write, or write little, but they continue to exert great influence over today's theatre. Their plays are seen as modern classics. In this group are Beckett (ill. 258), Genet (ill. 262-264), and Ionesco (ill. 267-270). Finally, among "political" authors, Gatti devotes himself more to political action than to theatrical writing, but Weiss comtinues to pursue his efforts at elucidation through dramaturgy (ill. 279-281).

Throughout this book, our emphasis will gradually shift toward new plays and new authors. But direction and scenography are no less attractive and important. How could we neglect, for example, the shock provoked by Victor Garcia's production of *The Balcony* (ill. 262-264), with its tower for the audience and its transparent spiral where the action takes place?

And how could we fail to admire the precise invention manifested by Japanese designers? For *Luminous Moss,* whose two acts take place in a grotto, then a court room, Kaoru Kanamori created a single, abstract setting: the walls and ceiling are pierced with holes which allow variations in the positions of the singers (ill. 277). And in *Echizen Bamboo Doll* Setsu Asakura realistically pictured a shipwreck.

In this light, we must evoke in some detail Vassiliev's *Yet the Dawns Here are Calm* (ill. 288), for its scenography is exemplary. The play concerns a female battalion sent to the front where the young women, each in her turn, are killed in the fighting. Here is Claudine Amiard-Chevrel's description *(Travail Théâtral,* no. XIV):

> There is a single, but modifiable, setting. At the rear and at both sides of the stage is hung a drop of gray-green tenting, covered with spots and full of holes. During the first part of the show, the body of a totally authentic military truck sits in the center. The women arrive in the rear and take their places, backs to the audience, creating the illusion of a military detachment, a convoy moving from day to night as the lighting shifts. They hit the ground during an aerial attack, lie in wait as if in a trench – the sound effects and the spots sweeping the auditorium create a vivid impression of battle. The truck becomes the shed in which the women are quartered, the bath where they wash. But when the German parachutists arrive, the truck breaks apart in the darkness, and its elements, each large enough to hide a body, are attached at one end to cables and suspended with the other end dragging along the stage. In this way they are used to suggest the boats used in traversing a swamp; a property attached to them evokes the world at the time of peace just before death; then an element leaves the shadows,turns over, giving up the frame and the characters of the past like a card in the hand of a conjurer.
>
> Most often, the elements figure the trees of the forest, between which the Germans – half-masks, half-shadows – and the Russians pursue each other in a tragic hide-and-seek to which the song of the birds lends a lyrical counterpoint. In the end, when the adjutant, alone in the half-shadows, wanders about mourning his dead soldiers, the elements turn in the rhythm of a sad waltz, like so many coffins in a macabre dance.

The generation of authors now 40 to 50 years old might easily be said to be dominated by Pinter. This is because his formal experiments with language – as instrument of domination, disintegration and depersonalization – appear to be an indispensable link between, let's say, Ionesco and Handke. But one could easily prefer Arrabal (ill. 343-344) or Dorst (ill. 298-305).

Perhaps it is possible to group these authors into sub-categories? Bond (ill. 355-356), Terson (ill. 347), Wesker (ill. 348) and Whitehead (ill. 349) surely all have things in common, most notably their modest social origins. And their insistence on observing the life of the humble classes is shared by Planchon (ill. 339-342) who, without ceasing to be a theatre manager and an innovative director, continues to write his own plays. Finally, despite fundamentally different conditions, we can see these same preoccupations in Heiner Müller (ill. 324-328) and Bokarev (ill. 353-354).

Of these authors, Dario Fo deserves a chapter apart, for his story has long been misunderstood. Like his compatriot De Filippo, he achieves commercial success. De Filippo gave new life to Neapolitan popular comedy; yet it took long years before he could be seen as more than a low-class entertainer. Fo, too, is an entertainer who packs houses, but his evolution, although logical, is very complex. He began by mounting revues with Parenti and Durano. Then, working with Franca Rame, he wrote and acted in farces, and then spectacular comedies which gained him an international reputation. At the height of his fame he disavowed his own repertory and undertook political theatre efforts in collaboration with the Italian Communist Party. Finally, in 1970, he broke with the Party, and founded *La Commune,* his own collective. His productions change with the currents of daily experience and in contact with local political and social circumstances. In this sense they are neither transmittable or translatable. His is not really "street theatre", but very exactly a "theatre of intervention".

While they don't really constitute a sub-category, an air of similarity brings together André Gregory, Joseph Chaikin and Robert Wilson (ill. 405). Their efforts all involve an open dramaturgy which raises fresh questions about the traditional role of the "author" and are based, *mutatis mutandis,* on collective creation. All three are American. Is that merely a coincidence?

Roger Planchon tendered indirect hommage to Bob Wilson when he said to *Le Monde*:

We are witnessing a theatrical springtime... When I began to work, it was the novel which counted and the theatre seemed to be a subproduct of literature. But now I believe, for example, that some of the experiments of the surrealists have reached maturity in the work of Bob Wilson. Faced with Bob Wilson, a writer is forced to realize that things have changed...

This theatrical springtime is astonishing because authentic poets have appeared on the stage... There have been no manifestos, just production-manifestos which attacked all that the theatre was... Bob Wilson, Grotowski, Peter Schumann, are all important, it seems to me, precisely because they are truly revolutionary.

Not knowing their work well enough, we shall not try to classify the Japanese authors, Moroi (ill. 330) and Inoue (ill. 357-362), or the Rumanian Popovici (ill. 331) or the Yugoslav Jovanovic (ill. 345).

Rezvani (ill. 317) is merely one of the leaders of a band of young French authors (Adrien, Benedetto, Grumberg, Hallet, Kraemer, Michel) often produced in the provinces as in Paris from 1970-1975, who have helped to give new tonalities to the political theatre.

By contrast, Derek Walcott (ill. 334), a West-Indian playwright, works in isolation; yet he has acquired little by little an international reputation through works of an undeniable quality.

Before moving on to the next generation of playwrights, we must deal briefly with Ballet. Here our scope is truly limited, to three leaders in dance whose status has been confirmed between 1970-1975. Alvin Ailey (ill. 335-338) continues to turn out a seemingly inexhaustible series of successes, without ever ceasing to create new choreographic visions. Maurice Béjart (ill. 289-294) shows a constant fecundity. And Alwin Nikolais (ill. 271-275) pursues, in *Triple Duo,* the formal experiments undertaken previously in, for example, *Allegory,* or, more recently, *Galaxy.*

Yet place ought to have been found for Merce Cunningham, surely, and Paul Taylor. And for the more recent choreographers: Hans van Manen, Peter Dockley, and so many others.

It is among the group of playwrights aged 30-40 that we find the most original experiments in dramaturgy.

Some, like Adri Boon (ill. 369), have mastered, as only the theatre's younger generation could, the as yet not fully explored resources of audio-visual technology (recording tape, video tape, etc.) and the magic of electronics.

Others, such as Handke (ill. 394-396), pose anew the problem of communication, particularly verbal communication. It is as yet too early to judge, but the next few years may see a true renaissance in the theatre of language, a renaissance totally opposed to the traditionally literary play. Already, Genet, Arrabal, Bond and De Boer (ill. 370-373) have stopped using language in the ways it had been used before them. As diverse as is their writing, they have all rejected Aristotelian rhetoric. In *Jumpers* (ill. 378), Tom Stoppard completely "disorients" speech. Yet, from discourse itself, artistic attention has turned most often to a scrutinization of the *Word,* the word in its pure state – sometimes the word being born (Handke's *Kaspar*).

Some recent reflections on the *Word* :

> Planchon: I wished to describe an image, but suddenly the words themselves took over. I found something was happening between them. I found they had a life of their own. While composing two speeches, I asked myself: what is this jump from one speech to another? It was this jump which preoccupied me, but also that space in the text through which, perhaps, poetry infilters.

> An extract from the program for *Orghast* (ill. 295-296): What is the relation between verbal and non-verbal theatre? What happens when gesture and sound turn into word? What is the exact place of the word in theatrical expression? As vibration? Concept? Music? Is any evidence buried in the sound structure of any ancient languages?

> And, already, in his *Empty Space* (¹), Peter Brook had wondered: Is there a language of actions – a language of word-as-part-of-movement, of word-as-lie, word-as-parody, of word-as-rubbish, of word as contradiction, of word-shock or word-cry?

> Jean-Pierre Vincent on Brook's work with *Timon of Athens* (ill. 57-63): In a Shakespearian phrase the meaning rests on an almost uninter-

---

(¹) Peter Brook: *The Empty Space* (London: MacGibbon and Kee, 1968).

rupted chain of key words which radiate their connotations, which react and rebound to and against each other. (...) The actor must fully play each image, even at the risk of dealing with the image out of all context. He must totally invest himself in the image during the time it occupies his vocal apparatus. This is the sole means for humanly raising oneself to the level of such a rich text: the constant variety of the text's images, thus realized by the imagination of the actor, assures that the development of the role will have an extreme density, but a density which changes with the material of the text. What a difference between this and our 19th Century tradition – in which the character exhibits a plausible behaviour and has a language compatible with his behaviour. Here, the character (and other things as well) exists only through the words he successively speaks.

Beyond this, a second stage is conceivable: the creation of new words, the invention of a new language for every play. What Michaux did with poetry, Serban, Brook with *Orghast* and Baal with *I* (ill. 391-393), are seeking to do in the theatre.

It only remains for us to deal with innovations in theatrical space.
Cultural protest finds its double in architectural protest. In 1968, the iconoclasts cast doubt on the value and pertinence of cultural institutions. Yet, as far as physical structures were concerned, the usefulness of the polyvalent theatre continued to be unquestioned for a time – thinking of them as flexible, architects assumed they could be adapted to any kind of production.
We can list a number of ingenious solutions. Liviu Ciulei's transformation of the Lucia Sturdza Bulandra Theatre's Studio for the production of *Power and Truth* (ill. 331) constitutes a fluid proposition which escapes all monotony. It permits proscenium staging, thrust (audience on three sides), and central (audience on two or four sides) staging. Ciulei describes it as follows:

1. Central stage (portable panels which fold up with the aid of winches) above the orchestra of the Italianate house. Height: +1.20 m; playing area: 9 x 10 m.
2. Transportable metallic frame which supports the central stage. For the proscenium arrangement, the frames are set under the panels which are folded up against the walls.
3. Transportable metal girder.
4. Mobile bleachers divided into three sections.
5. Permanent cat-walk either for spectators or lighting.
6. Proscenium space adjoining the central stage. Height: ±0.00 m. Can be utilized: a) as a prolongation of the central stage, at the same height (+1.20 m). Total playing area: 9 x 15 m; b) for the installation of ramps, stairways, units, etc.; c) for the installation of supplementary bleachers.
7. Portable bleachers at a heigh of +2,35 m above the proscenium stage. (They may also be placed at ±0.00 m).
8. Passageway for set pieces and access for actors under the bleachers.

9. Portable stairways and walk-ways.
10. Permanent stairways and walk-ways.
11. Principal access for the audience.
12. Orchestra of the proscenium house.
13. Amphitheatre of the proscenium house.

But a growing number of theatre people are leaving theatrical spaces entirely. From 1970-1975, more and more small groups descend into the street, invade the schools or the department stores and seek to discover potential spectators in the very spaces where they work.
Some important productions, created by lasting collectives, stand out from this abundant mass.
Such as the Grand Magic Circus (ill. 374-375 and 397-404), about which Jérôme Savary writes:
> The Magic Circus is characterized by the fact that it *plays* with pleasure... There is no written text... The group itself collectively constructs its characters, its gags, its interferences... The Circus itself composes the music. We reject the tape recorder... A boring production, to my mind, can not be a good one... For us, the theatre is lived from day to day and rewrites itself each evening.

The Magic Circus attracts a heterogeneous group of spectators which a production like *From Moses to Mao* unites in the experience of pleasure. "A derisory and mournful account of man's knowledge of his own history", writes Alain Leblanc in *Le Quotidien*. "*From Moses to Mao* is a child's look – a strangely lucid look which inspires a sneaky laugh – at history as it is consciously magnified and simplified by the textbooks, in which there is only progress, victories and, most often, accumulations of horrors and stupidities".
The productions of the Magic Circus are presented anywhere, rarely in a traditional theatre and most often inside a tent.

For its part, the *Théâtre du Soleil* has occupied for five years the Cartoucherie de Vincennes in the outskirts of Paris. To this day it has presented three productions there: *1789 (The Revolution Must End With the Perfection of Happiness)*, *1793 (The Revolutionary City Belongs to this World)* and *The Age of Gold*.
Both created by the same collective, the first two complete each other through their oppositions. Ariane Mnouchkine describes them as follows: "In *1789*, the actors play jugglers who act out stories of the Revolution. In *1793* the actors play the *sans-culottes* who recall the Revolution for themselves". In both cases, historical events are seen from the popular point of view, as the people might imagine, feel, live and suffer the Revolution.
The productions of the *Théâtre du Soleil* are typical of the 1970s: they are not presented in a theatre, the text didn't exist prior to the production, the acting, seemingly improvised, is consciously coarse and rejects the subtleties of psychology.

The miracle is that this accumulation of "rejections" (of theatre structure, psychology, etc.) leads to a rigorous dramaturgy, a strict economy of means, and to an exceptionally polished technical production.
I witnessed a performance of *1793* on a bright sunny afternoon. During the first third of the show, I was overwhelmed to see how the rays of sun pouring through the windows illuminated, by some marvelous chance, just those areas which needed light! Suddenly I understood that the "sun" was artificial.
Denis Bablet describes the genesis of this effect (*Travail Théâtral*, no. IX):
> What were the problems involved in lighting *1793*? The members of the Théâtre du Soleil had not failed to notice the beautiful, luminous atmosphere of the Cartoucherie when the gentle bluish light falling from the upper skylight mixed with the more golden beams of sun piercing the windows. They decided to try to recreate this interior daylight...
> The effect of the skylight posed the trickiest difficulties. To obtain the equivalent of daylight, the Théâtre du Soleil technicians chose fluorescent tubes reflected by a white surface. 300 tubes were used, grouped in twos on 150 modules. The arrangement of these modules along the frame of the skylight, and their installation behind a metal shield, kept them from being visible to the public. Each 40 watt tube was 1.20 m long. But a reflective surface still had to be found which would create no shadow zones, yet whose curve would be sufficiently restricted so as not to cause anchoring problems. Shiny paint was rejected for technical reasons, and the use of movie screens proved

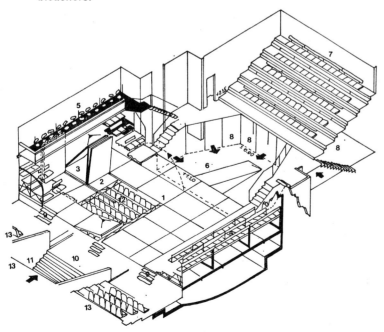

Arrangement of the Studio of the Lucia Sturdza Bulandra Theatre.

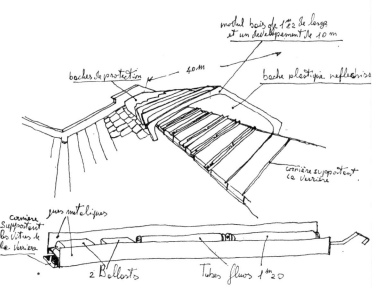

The arrangement for the lighting from the skylight in *1793* (drawing by Ro
Moscoso).

financially prohibitive. Finally, the technicians decided to use pl
truck tarpaulins, with their relatively dull surface. stretched
33 units. These were then covered with construction tarps w
in turn were backed by painters' tarps – the whole held in plac
1000 meters of steel cable.
This design was hardly justified by a desire for simplicity, foi
fluorescent tubes created great control difficulties. The warr
problem, which was dependent on the ever-changing outside temp
ture, had to be solved, and this necessitated the use of interme
potentiometers. And delicate control was required, to allow
lighting to develop from a faint glow : this demanded the constru

Zartan
by the Grand Magic Circus
and its Sad Animals.

KEY TO THE CAPTIONS
ACCOMPANYING
THE ILLUSTRATIONS

THE DRAMA : □

First : Author's name; year of birth and, if
applicable, death; adapter's name if his
contribution has been significant.

Next : Title in its original language.

1. Name of the director.
2. Name of the designer.
3. Name of the costume designer.
4. Name of the choreographer.
5. Name of the composer.
6. Name of the company and/or theatre,
   followed by the city and the year of production.
7. Name of the photographer.

OPERA – MUSICAL THEATRE : ○
THE DANCE : △

First : Composer's name; year of birth and,
if applicable, death.

Next : Title in its original language.

1. Name of the director.
2. Name of the designer.
3. Name of the costume designer.
4. Name of the choreographer.
5. Name of the librettist, the author of any
   texts, or the author whose work has been
   used for the libretto.
6. Name of the company and/or theatre,
   followed by the city and the year of production.
7. Name of the photographer.

KEYS TO THIS WORK

The illustrations are organized in chronological order by author for the drama, and by composer for the musical theatre and the dance. The different genres are designated by a symbol preceding the caption:

□ *the drama,*

○ *musical theatre,*

△ *the dance.*

The captions are edited in accordance with a code which makes them international.

First of all, the title of a work is given in its original language. For example : for The Children of the Sun *by Gorki, presented in Prague, we have used the original Russian title* Dieti Solntsa *rather than its Czech equivalent. Similarly, Peter Handke's* The Ride Over Lake Constance, *presented in France, is found with its German title,* Der Ritt über den Bodensee. *English translations of these titles may be found in the index.*

When the original work – whether it be a play or a novel – has been significantly modified by an adapter, we use the original title of the adaptation, with the original title of the work following between brackets. Thus, Dostoevski's The Brothers Karamazov, *adapted for the theatre by the Yugoslav director Bajcetic, is designated as* Sladostrasnici Karamazovi (Bratia Karamazov).

When a city is the capital of its country, we thought it unnecessary to follow it with the country's name – as with Praha, Bern or Tokyo. After non-capital cities, the country's name is found between brackets. In some cases, the name of the country may be unfamiliar : Finland is «Suomi», the German Democratic Republic is "D.D.R." (Deutsche Demokratische Republik), the German Federal Republic becomes "B.R.D." (Bundesrepublik Deutschland), Switzerland is "Helvetia", etc.

We include between brackets under no.1 the names of the directors who should be considered as the coordinators of a collective production.

1 – □ – **AISCHYLOS** (525-456): ORESTEIA. 1: Luca Ronconi. 2-3: Enrico Job. 4: Marise Flach – Angelo Corti. 6: Cooperativa Tuscolano. Chiesa di San Niccolo. Spoleto (Italia). 1973. 7: Marcello Norberth.

AGAMEMNON. Cassandra on Agamemnon's chariot (Episode 4).

The universe of AGAMEMNON is vague, unformed; the characters move in a cosmic, almost extra-terrestrial space. In contrast, the action of THE CHOEPHORI takes place entirely between four walls, while THE EUMENIDES unfolds in a futuristic city.
(Luca Ronconi)

AGAMEMNON. Cassandre sur le char d'Agamemnon (Episode 4).

L'univers de l'AGAMEMNON est informe, les personnages se meuvent dans une région cosmique presque sidérale; au contraire, l'action des CHOÉPHORES se passe toute entre 4 murs; tandis que les EUMÉNIDES se déroulent dans une ville futuriste.
(Luca Ronconi)

1

2

3

2/4 – □ – AISCHYLOS (525-456):
ORESTEIA. 1: Luca Ronconi.
2-3: Enrico Job. 4: Marise Flach –
Angelo Corti. 6: Cooperativa
Tuscolano. Cinema Arsenale. Venezia
(Italia). 1972. 7: ASAC.

*2. AGAMEMNON. **The chorus
evokes the predictions of Calchas
and the sacrifice of Iphigenia
(Parodos).***
*3. THE CHOEPHORI. **The
chorus of libation-bearers await
Electra. The scenic structure with
the upper platform lowered.***
*4. THE EUMENIDES. **The
arrival of Orestes in Athens
(Episode 1).***

2. AGAMEMNON. Le chœur évoque
les prédictions de Calchas et le
sacrifice d'Iphigénie (Parodos).
3. LES CHOÉPHORES. Les
Choéphores attendent Electre. Le
dispositif scénique avec la plate-forme
supérieure abaissée.
4. LES EUMÉNIDES. L'arrivée
d'Oreste à Athènes (Episode 1).

5

5/7 – □ – AISCHYLOS (525-456):
ORESTEIA. 1: Luca Ronconi.
2-3: Enrico Job. 4: Marise Flach –
Angelo Corti. 6: Cooperativa
Tuscolano. Chiesa di San Niccolo.
Spoleto (Italia). 1973.
7: Marcello Norberth.

*5. AGAMEMNON. **Helen's boat
(Stasimon 2). A member of the
chorus carries the statue of Venus.***
*6. THE CHOEPHORI. **Electra
with the libation-bearers (Episode 1).***
*7. THE EUMENIDES. **Orestes
with Athena (Episode 2).***

5. AGAMEMNON. La barque
d'Hélène (Stasimon 2). Un choreute
porte la statue de Vénus.
6. LES CHOÉPHORES. Electre avec
les Choéphores (Episode 1).
7. LES EUMÉNIDES. Oreste et
Athéna (Episode 2).

6

7

8/10 – □ – **SOPHOCLES** (496-406) –
YANNIS RITSOS : ELEKTRA.
1 : Antoine Vitez. 2-3 : Yannis Kokkos.
6 : Théâtre des Quartiers d'Ivry –
Théâtre des Amandiers. Nanterre.
(France). 1971. 7 : Nicolas Treatt.

We abandon all naturalism in the
acting : the actors play not merely
the «situation», but the dream of the
situation; I mean : how this or that
moment will appear tomorrow, for
one character or another, in his
dreams.
(Antoine Vitez)

Nous refusons tout naturalisme dans
le jeu : les acteurs ne jouent pas
seulement « la situation », mais le
rêve de la situation, je veux dire :
comment tel ou tel moment appa-
raîtra demain, pour celui-ci ou
celle-là, dans ses rêves.
(Antoine Vitez)

11 – □ – **SOPHOCLES** (496-406) –
ANDREI SERBAN : ELEKTRA.
1-2 : Andreï Serban. 3 : Eliane Gariano.
5 : Catherine Mueller. 6 : Octobre à
Bordeaux – La Mamma. Festival
d'Automne. Sainte Chapelle. Paris.
1973. 7 : Michel Berger.

12 – □ – **SOPHOCLES** (496-406) –
HEINER MÜLLER :
PHILOCTETES.
1 : Miro Medimorec. 2 : Drago Turina.
3 : Marija Zarak. 4 : Ivica Boban.
5 : Arpad Barath.
6 : Teatar I TD. Zagreb
(Jugoslavija). 1972.
7 : Zeljko Stojanovic.

11

12

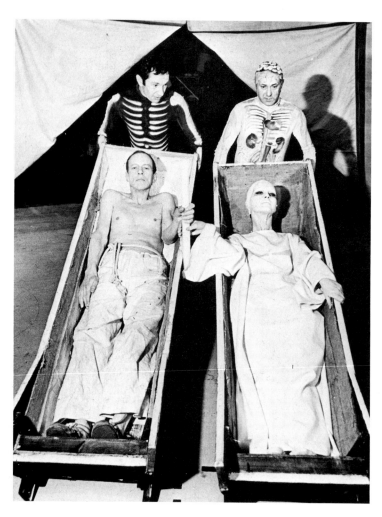

13/14 – □ – **DANTE ALIGHIERI** (1265-1321) – **JOZEF SZAJNA** : DANTE (DIVINA COMMEDIA).
1-2-3: Jozef Szajna.
5: Krzysztof Penderecki.
6: Teatr Studio. Warszawa. 1972.
7: Stefan Okolowicz.

Three large wheels, limned with phosphorescent light, roll across the revolving stage. Charon ties the artist, the eternal wanderer, to one, the second is assigned to the bestial Cerberus, the third to Beatrice, the personification of death.
(Elzbieta Morawiec. The Theatre in Poland)

Trois grands cercles entourés d'un halo phosphorescent roulent sur la scène tournante; au premier, Charon enchaîne l'artiste, éternel pèlerin, le second est destiné au monstrueux Cerbère et le troisième à Béatrice qui incarne la Mort.
(Elzbieta Morawiec. Le Théâtre en Pologne)

15/17 – ☐ – **NICCOLO MACHIAVELLI** (1469-1527): MANDRAGOLA.
1: Paulo Magelli. 2: Dusan Ristic.
3: Ljerka Kalcic. 5: Mario Relini.
6: Narodno pozoriste. Beograd. 1972.
7: Dragoljub Kazic (15) – Miroslav Krstic (16/17).

At the end of the production, the Christ opens up and becomes a music box adorned with small, multicolored lights.
(Dusan Ristic)

A la fin du spectacle, le Christ s'ouvre et devient boîte à musique ornée de petites lampes multi-colores.
(Dusan Ristic)

18 – □ – WILLIAM SHAKESPEARE
(1564-1616): RICHARD II.
1: John Barton. 2-3: Timothy O'Brien
– Tazeena Firth. 5: James Walker.
6: Royal Shakespeare Company.
Royal Shakespeare Theatre.
Stratford-upon-Avon (U.K.). 1973.
7: Sophie Baker.

19 – □ – WILLIAM SHAKESPEARE
(1564-1616): RICHARD III.
1: Manfred Wekwerth.
2-3: Andreas Reinhardt –
Johanna Kieling. 5: Günther Fischer.
6: Deutsches Theater. Berlin D.D.R.
1972. 7: Maria Steinfeldt.

20/21 – □ – WILLIAM
SHAKESPEARE (1564-1616) –
FRIEDRICH DÜRRENMATT :
KING JOHN. 1: Dieter Stürmer.
2-3: Ulrich E. Milatz.
6: Stadttheater. Bern. 1972.
7: Sandra Sibiglia.

22 – □ – WILLIAM SHAKESPEARE
(1564-1616): THE MERCHANT OF
VENICE. 1: Peter Zadek.
2: René Allio. 3: Christine Laurent.
5: Peer Raaben.
6: Schauspielhaus. Bochum (BRD).
1973. 7: Ilse Buhs.

19

20

21

22

23 – ☐ – WILLIAM SHAKESPEARE
(1564-1616): AS YOU LIKE IT.
1: Jim Sharman. 2-3: Brian Thompson.
4: Keith Bain. 5: Sandra McKenzie.
6: Old Tote Theatre Company.
Parade Theatre. Sydney (Australia).
1971. 7: Grant Mudford.

Jim Sharman saw Shakespeare's
fable of injustice within a wordly
court set off by a life of natural peace
in the Forest of Arden as an allegory
of the revolt of the early 1970's
against the conventions of the older
generation.

Shakespeare oppose l'injustice du
monde et de la Cour à la paix
naturelle de la Forêt d'Arden.
Pour Jim Sharman, c'est une allé-
gorie de la révolte de 68 contre les
conventions de la vieille génération.

24 – ☐ – WILLIAM SHAKESPEARE
(1564-1616): THE TAMING OF THE
SHREW. 1: Robin Lovejoy.
2-3: Anne Frazer. 5: Sandra McKenzie.
6: Old Tote Theatre Company.
Parade Theatre. Sydney (Australia).
1972. 7: Grant Mudford.

Twin revolving stages, while static,
represented the verandah of a farm
house. When turned they provided
a myriad of combinations pacing the
action to dancing comedy as the
suspension of disbelief prevailed
upon Sly and the theatre patrons.

Deux scènes tournantes à l'arrêt
représentent la véranda d'une
maison de campagne. En tournant,
elles donnent lieu à d'innombrables
combinaisons, l'action prend le
rythme d'une comédie dansante,
l'incrédulité s'estompe chez Sly et
les spectateurs...

25 – ☐ – WILLIAM SHAKESPEARE
(1564-1616): HAMLET.
1: Senne Rouffaer. 2-3: Serge Creuz.
6: Koninklijke Vlaamse Schouwburg.
Brussel. 1972. 7: Serge Creuz.

26/30 – ☐ – **WILLIAM SHAKESPEARE** (1564-1616): HAMLET. 1: Yourij Lioubimov. 2-3: David Borovskij. 5: Yourij Boutzko.
6: Moskovskij Teatr Dramy i Komedii na Taganke. Moskva. 1972.
7: S. Tchernov.

...a wall of limed bricks as a background and several wooden buttresses. A woolen curtain, able to be moved in all directions, organizes the space differently for each scene by varying its relation to the actors.
(David Borovskij)

Un mur de briques chaulées pour fond et quelques soutènements de bois... Un rideau de laine qui se déplace dans toutes les directions organise d'une manière chaque fois différente l'espace, variant ses rapports avec les acteurs.
(David Borovskij)

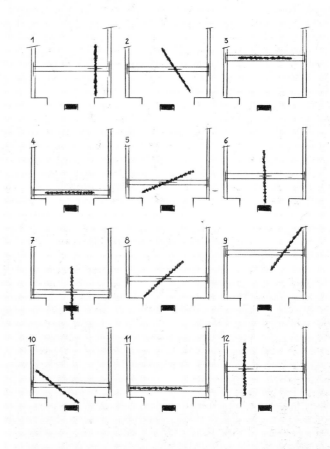

30

31/35 – ☐ – **WILLIAM SHAKESPEARE** (1564-1616): MEASURE FOR MEASURE.
1: André Steiger. 2-3: Claude Lemaire.
6: Théâtre du Parvis. Bruxelles. 1972.
7: Jean-Paul Hubin.

Moral rationales, psychological conflicts, individual modes of behaviour hide with an illusory mask, an adulterated disguise, the reality of political machinations.
(André Steiger)

Les justifications morales, les conflits psychologiques, les conduites individualistes recouvrent d'un masque illusoire, d'un déguisement frelaté la réalité des manipulations politiques.
(André Steiger)

33

34

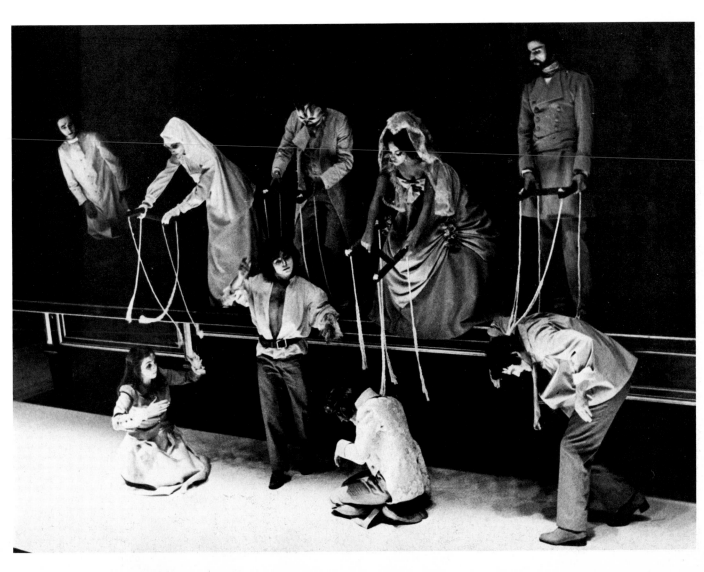

35

36/38 – □ – WILLIAM SHAKESPEARE (1564-1616): MEASURE FOR MEASURE.
1: Dinu Cernescu.
2: Dinu Cernescu – Sorin Haber.
3: Sorin Haber. 5: Stefan Zorzor.
6: Teatrul Giulesti. Bucuresti. 1971.
7: Scinteii.

During the course of the action the form of the actor changes... In the first scene, Angelo wears a seminarian's garb and carries a book under his arm; nearsighted, wearing glasses, he hesitates at each word. A single scene suffices for his secret desires to modify his outward appearance.
(Dinu Cernescu)

Au cours de l'action, la forme de l'acteur se modifie... Pendant le premier tableau, Angelo est habillé d'un costume de séminariste, avec un livre sous le bras, myope, portant lunettes, il hésite à chaque mot. Un seul tableau suffit pour que ses désirs secrets modifient son aspect.
(Dinu Cernescu)

36

37

38

39/41 – □ – **WILLIAM SHAKESPEARE** (1564-1616): KING LEAR. 1: Kalle Holmberg. 2: Juha Lukala. 3: Mans Hedström. 6: Turun Kaupunginteatteri. Turku (Suomi). 1972. 7: Studio Rex.

39

40

41

...a great theatre of fools, a huge «circus-world», a cosmic arena for the representation of life and history. (Giorgio Strehler)

...Un grand théâtre de fous, un grand « monde-cirque », une piste cosmique pour la représentation de la vie et de l'histoire. (Giorgio Strehler)

SHAKESPEARE (1564-1616):
KING LEAR. 1: Giorgio Strehler.
2-3: Ezio Frigerio. 4: Marise Flach.
5: Fiorenzo Carpi. 6: Piccolo Teatro
di Milano. Teatro Metastasio. Prato
(Italia). 1973.
7: Tommaso Le Pera (42) –
Luigi Ciminaghi (43/45).

The performance unfolds within a
circular drop stretched and held by
ropes, a truncated big-top which
defines an arena. A strange material
– blackish, shiny gravel, which
hasn't the weight nor the density
of stone – suggests in its lightness
the sawdust men spread over the
floor of the circus.
(François Truan. Travail Théâtral)

La représentation se déroule à
l'intérieur d'une toile circulaire
tendue et maintenue par des
cordes, un chapiteau tronqué qui
délimite une piste : un étrange
matériau, gravier noirâtre et
scintillant qui n'a ni la pesanteur,
ni la densité du minéral, rappelle,
par sa légèreté, la sciure que
répandent les hommes de piste sur
l'arène du cirque.
(François Truan. Travail Théâtral)

44

45

46

47

48

49

50

51

52

46 – □ – WILLIAM SHAKESPEARE
(1564-1616): CORIOLANUS.
1: Trevor Nunn – Buzz Goodbody –
Evan Smith. 2-3: Christopher Morley –
Ann Curtis. 5: Guy Woolfenden.
6: Royal Shakespeare Company.
Royal Shakespeare Theatre.
Stratford-upon-Avon (U.K.). 1972.
7: Reg Wilson.

**47/52 – □ – WILLIAM
SHAKESPEARE** (1564-1616) –
HEINER MÜLLER : MACBETH.
1: Petar Vecek. 2: Drago Turina.
3: Ingrid Begovic. 5: Branco Vodenicar.
6: Teatar I TD. Zagreb
(Jugloslavija). 1974.
7: Zeljko Stojanovic.

*The motives of Shakespeare's
characters are clarified in Heiner
Müller's version by the addition of
peasants and soldiers.*

Les mobiles des personnages de
Shakespeare s'éclairent, dans la
version de Heiner Müller, par
l'adjonction de paysans et de soldats.

53 – □ – WILLIAM SHAKESPEARE
(1564-1616): PERICLES.
1: Frank Dunlop. 2-3: Jean-Marie
Fievez. 6: Théâtre National de
Belgique. Bruxelles. 1973.
7: Guido Marcon.

*The action is set on an imaginary
Mediterranean beach, to which a
comic bowler-hatted entertainer
(Gower) comes to amuse the holiday-
makers and draws them into enacting
themselves this story of love frustrated
by the shipwreck.
(Ossia Trilling. The Stage)*

Frank Dunlop situe l'action sur une
plage imaginaire de la Méditerranée
où un amuseur coiffé d'un chapeau
melon vient divertir les vacanciers
et les conduit à représenter eux-
mêmes cette histoire d'amour
compromise par un naufrage.
(Ossia Trilling. The Stage)

**54/56 – □ – WILLIAM
SHAKESPEARE** (1564-1616):
TIMON OF ATHENS.
1: Tomislav Radic. 2: Drago Turina.
3: Diana Kosec Bourek. 5: Bosko
Petrovic.
6: Hrvatsko narodno kazaliste.
Zagreb (Jugloslavija). 1973.
7: Robert Valai.

53

54

55

56

57/63 – □ – WILLIAM SHAKESPEARE (1564-1616):
TIMON OF ATHENS.
1: Peter Brook. 2-3: Michel Launay.
6: Théâtre des Bouffes du Nord.
Paris. 1974. 7: Michel Berger (57) –
Chantal Gaulin (59/63).

Out of an old italianate theatre, Peter Brook created a new theatrical space : the seats of the orchestra disappeared, to be replaced by a cement floor which serves as the main playing area; a removable wooden unit covered up the orchestra pit; the old raised stage gave way to a pit 20 feet deep... The decayed walls remain bare.

D'un vieux théâtre à l'italienne, Peter Brook a fait un nouveau lieu scénique : les sièges du parterre ont disparu, remplacés par une dalle de béton qui sert d'aire de jeu principale; la fosse d'orchestre est recouverte d'un plancher de bois amovible ; l'ancienne scène surélevée a fait place a une fosse de 6 m de profondeur... Les murs blessés se montrent à nu...

57

FOSSE

COULISSE

AIRE
DE
JEU

COULISSE

ESCALIER
VERS 1er
ETAGE

GRADINS POUR
SPECTATEURS

PORTE

PORTE

PORTE

PORTE

PORTE

PORTE

59

Faced with the decaying universe of Timon and the nascent world of Alcibiades, a vital question is raised: What is to be destroyed? What is to be saved?
(Peter Brook)

Devant l'univers entièrement saccagé de Timon et devant le monde naissant d'Alcibiade, une question vitale se pose; qu'est-ce qui est à détruire ? Qu'est-ce qui est à sauver ?
(Peter Brook)

60 /63

64/69 – ☐ – CHRISTOPHER MARLOWE (1564-1593): THE MASSACRE AT PARIS.
1: Patrice Chéreau. 2: Richard Peduzzi.
6: Théâtre National Populaire. Villeurbanne (France). 1972.
7: Claude Bricage.

The entire stage is a basin, 16 inches deep. Only certain elements emerge from the water, narrow quais in the back and on the sides.
Moreover, mobile sidewalks rolling on rails fixed to the basin's bottom and controlled from the wings by winches, can extend into the water carrying the actors.
(Richard Monod. Travail Théâtral)

Tout le plateau est un bassin de 40 cm de fond. Seules parties émergées fixes, des quais étroits au fond et sur les côtés; en outre, des trottoirs mobiles, manœuvrés des coulisses, à bras d'hommes, à l'aide de treuils et roulant sur des rails fixés au fond du bassin, peuvent avancer à fleur d'eau et porter les acteurs.
(Richard Monod. Travail Théâtral)

66

67

68

69

70 – □ – CHRISTOPHER MARLOWE (1564-1593): Dr. FAUSTUS. 1: Arieh Sachs. 2: Arie Navon. 3: Ruth Dar. 6: Hateatron Haleumi Habimah. Tel-Aviv. 1973. 7: Jaacov Agor.

The set was built in the form of an hour glass, meant to symbolise Dr. Faustus' race against time.

Le décor représente un sablier symbolisant la course du Dr. Faust contre le temps.

71/78 – □ – MOLIÈRE (1622-1673): TARTUFFE. 1: Roger Planchon. 2: Hubert Monloup. 3: Jacques Schmidt. 6: Théâtre National Populaire. Villeurbanne (France). 1974. 7: Rajak Ohanian (71/73) – Denis Gontard (74/78).

Orgon's recently acquired house – almost a palace – is in the midst of radical redecoration. The statues are gone, the columns are being reconstructured. Huge tarpaulins cover the walls.
(Michel Cournot. Le Monde)

La maison qu'Orgon vient d'acquérir – presque un palais – est en chantier. On a déposé des statues, on reconstruit des colonnes, d'immenses bâches recouvrent les murs.
(Michel Cournot. Le Monde)

70

71

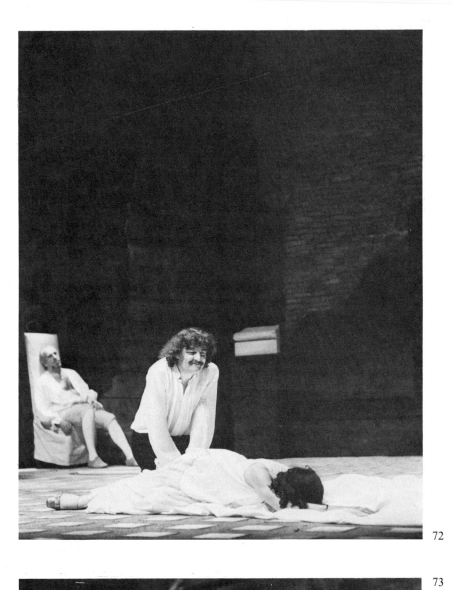

72

73

74/78

79

79 – □ – MOLIÈRE (1622-1673) – **TONY HARRISON :**
LE MISANTHROPE.
1: John Dexter.
2-3: Tanya Moiseiwitsch.
5: Marc Wilkinson. 6: National Theatre. Old Vic. London. 1973.

In Tony Harrison's jaunty translation, there are references to de Gaulle.

Dans l'adaptation désinvolte de Tony Harrison, on trouve des allusions à de Gaulle...

80/85 – □ – JEAN RACINE (1639-1699): PHÈDRE.
1: Albert-André Lheureux.
2-3: Elisabeth de Wée – Arik Joukovski.
5: Bernard Parmegiani – Lucie Vellere – Gustav Holst – Anton Bruckner – Antonio Vivaldi. 6: Forest National. Bruxelles. 1974.

I sought to turn PHEDRE into a sumptuous orchestra...
(Albert-André Lheureux)

J'ai voulu faire de PHÈDRE un orchestre somptueux.
(Albert-André Lheureux)

80/85

**86 – □ – MONZAEMON
CHIKAMATSU** (1653-1724) –
KOSUKE TATSUTA : UMEKAWA
– CHUBEI.
1-2: Akira Wakabayashi.
3: Susumu Takashima.
4: Kotama Yoshida. 5: Yoichi Shigeto.
6: Kokusai Seinen Engeki Centre.
Tokyo. 1974. 7: Chi Kashiwara.

*A modern singer appears in the
midst of traditional Bunraku
puppets.*

Une chanteuse moderne apparaît au
milieu des marionnettes tradition-
nelles du Bunraku.

86

87

87 – □ – MARIVAUX (1688-1763):
LES ACTEURS DE BONNE FOI.
1: Jacques Rosner. 2-3: Jacques Voizot.
5: Karin Trow. 6: Théâtre du
Lambrequin – Centre Dramatique du
Nord. Tourcoing. (France). 1973.

*In the white light of a skylight,
Jacques Rosner exposes the antagonism
of the dynamic bourgeoisie and the
reactionary aristocracy.*
(Colette Godard. Le Monde)

Sous l'éclairage blanc d'une ver-
rière, Jacques Rosner met en
lumière l'opposition de la bourgeoisie dynamique et de l'aristocra-
tie réactionnaire.
(Colette Godard. Le Monde)

88

89

90

88/93 – ☐ – **MARIVAUX** (1688-1763):
LA DISPUTE. 1: Patrice Chéreau.
2: Richard Peduzzi. 3: Jacques Schmidt.
6: Théâtre National Populaire.
Villeurbanne (France). 1973.
7: Claude Bricage.

*A courtyard, created and dominated
by tall, immaculate and strangely
timeless architectural forms (they are
renaissance and contemporary at the
same time), opens onto a dense forest,
which could provide either the possibility of escape or still another confinement.*
(Bernard Dort. Travail Théâtral)

Une cour, prise entre de hautes
architectures immaculées et
étrangement intemporelles (elles
sont de la Renaissance et
d'aujourd'hui à la fois), s'ouvre sur
une forêt épaisse dont on ne sait
trop si elle est une possibilité de
fuite ou une autre clôture.
(Bernard Dort. Travail Théâtral)

91

92

93

94/96 – ☐ – **VOLTAIRE** (1694-1778) –
**ROBERTO GUICCIARDINI –
GRUPPO DELLA ROCCA** :
VIAGGIO CONTROVERSO DI
CANDIDO E ALTRI NEGLI
ARCHIPELAGHI DELLA
RAGIONE (CANDIDE).
1 : Roberto Guicciardini.
2-3 : Lorenzo Ghiglia. 5 : Guido
Mariani. 6 : Il Gruppo della Rocca di
Firenze. Teatro La Fenice. Venezia
(Italia). 1971. 7 : Asac.

*This theatrical version of CANDIDE
involves more than a simple scenic
transposition of Voltaire's celebrated
novel : numerous elements drawn
from contemporary literature served
in the creation of the production.
(Roberto Guicciardini)*

L'élaboration de ce CANDIDE ne se
résume pas en une simple transposition scénique du célèbre roman;
de nombreux matériaux tirés de la
littérature contemporaine ont servi
à la définition du spectacle.
(Roberto Guicciardini)

97 – ☐ – **CARLO GOLDONI**
(1707-1793): L'AMANTE
MILITARE. 1 : Charles Joris.
2-3 : Bernard Billa. 5 : Guy Bovet.
6 : Théâtre Populaire Romand.
La Chaux-de-Fonds (Helvetia). 1973.
7 : Maryvonne Freitag.

98 – ☐ – **CARLO GOLDONI**
(1707-1793): LE BARUFFE
CHIOZZOTTE. 1 : Paulo Magelli.
2 : Dusan Ristic. 3 : Ljerka Kalcic.
5 : Vojislav Kostic.
6 : Narodno pozoriste. Beograd. 1973.
7 : Miroslav Krstic.

*The decor, mounted on wheels,
turns in all directions. The actors
themselves shift it from the inside.
At the end of the production an
enormous fan appears, controlled
by an actor. All is caught up in its
wind : houses, objects, hats and
bonnets. The white backdrop
becomes a sail and disappears into
the black hole of backstage.
(Dusan Ristic)*

Le décor, monté sur roues, tourne
dans toutes les directions. Les
acteurs eux-mêmes le déplacent de
l'intérieur des éléments. A la fin du
spectacle apparaît un ventilateur
énorme dirigé par un acteur. Tout
est emporté : maisons, objets,
chapeaux et bonnets. La toile de
fond, toute blanche, devient une
voile de bateau et disparaît dans le
trou noir de l'arrière-scène.
(Dusan Ristic)

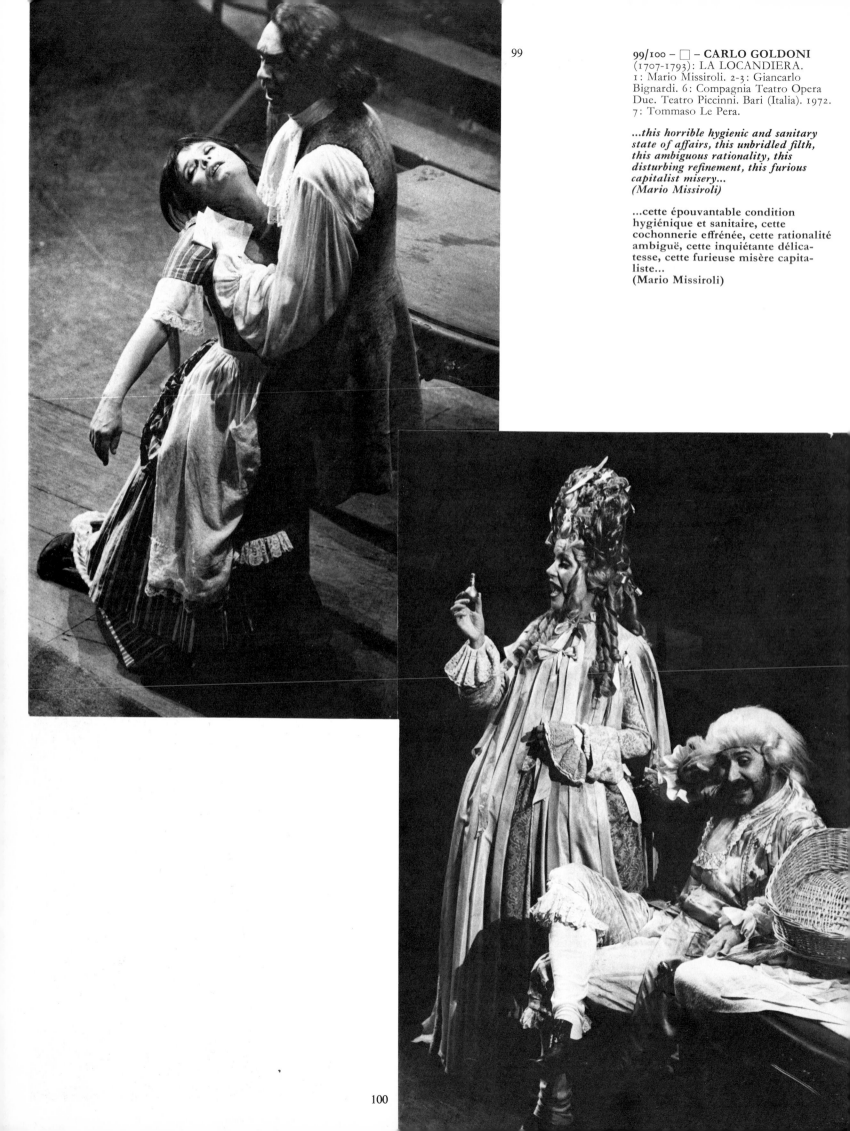

99/100 – □ – **CARLO GOLDONI**
(1707-1793): LA LOCANDIERA.
1: Mario Missiroli. 2-3: Giancarlo
Bignardi. 6: Compagnia Teatro Opera
Due. Teatro Piccinni. Bari (Italia). 1972.
7: Tommaso Le Pera.

*...this horrible hygienic and sanitary
state of affairs, this unbridled filth,
this ambiguous rationality, this
disturbing refinement, this furious
capitalist misery...*
(Mario Missiroli)

...cette épouvantable condition
hygiénique et sanitaire, cette
cochonnerie effrénée, cette rationalité
ambiguë, cette inquiétante délica-
tesse, cette furieuse misère capita-
liste...
(Mario Missiroli)

101

101 – ○ – JOSEPH HAYDN
(1732-1809): LE PESCATRICI.
1: Andreas Meyer-Hanno.
2: Ary Oechslin. 3: Brigitte Lenz.
5: Carlo Goldoni.
6: Stadttheater. Bern. 1971.
7: Willi Gasché.

102 – □ – DONATIEN DE SADE
(1740-1814) – **GIULIANO**
VASILICO: LE 120 GIORNATE DI
SODOMA (LES CENT VINGT
JOURNÉES DE SODOME).
1: Giuliano Vasilico
2-3: Angelo delle Piane –
Agostino Raff. 5: Agostino Raff –
Alvin Curran. 6: Beat 72. Roma. 1972.
7: Agnese De Donato.

102

103

104

105

103/105 – □ – **JOHANN WOLFGANG GOETHE**
(1749-1832): FAUST.
1-2-3: Jozef Szajna.
5: Boguslaw Schäffer.
6: Teatr Polski. Warszawa. 1974.
7: Franciszek Myszkowski.

A tragedy of the man who struggles in solitude with himself, a man who seeks to combat his own weakness.
(Jozef Szajna)

Une tragédie de l'homme qui lutte dans la solitude avec lui-même, un homme qui essaie de combattre ses propres impuissances.
(Jozef Szajna)

106/112 – ○ – WOLFGANG AMADEUS MOZART (1756-1791): DIE ZAUBERFLÖTE.
1: Giorgio Strehler. 2-3: Luciano Damiani. 5: J.E. Schikaneder. 6: Grosses Festspielhaus. Salzburger Festspiele. Salzburg (Österreich). 1974.

A vast, bare space, shining like an icy surface, barren and esoteric, limited in the distance by a drop, the symbol of the celestial dome. The drop is raised occasionally to form triangular openings which let through certain elements of the setting, or the choruses, messengers bearing the secrets of the universe. (Jacques Lonchampt. Le Monde)

Un vaste espace nu, brillant comme une surface glacée, désertique et ésotérique, limité au loin par une toile, symbole de la coupole céleste; elle se soulève par moments en triangles qui laissent passer tels éléments de décor ou les chœurs, messagers des secrets de l'univers. (Jacques Lonchampt. Le Monde)

111

112

113/114 – ○ – **WOLFGANG AMADEUS MOZART** (1756-1791): DON GIOVANNI.
1-2-3: Franco Zeffirelli.
5: Lorenzo da Ponte.
6: Staatsoper. Wien. 1972.
7: Elisabeth Hausmann.

115

116

115/117 – □ – **FRIEDRICH SCHILLER** (1759-1805): KABALE UND LIEBE.
1: Klaus Erforth – Alexander Stillmark.
2-3: Jochen Finke.
6: Kammerspiele des Deutschen Theaters. Berlin D.D.R. 1972.
7: Cecilie Münchhausen (115/116) – Gisela Brandt (117).

117

118/123 – □ – **FRIEDRICH
SCHILLER** (1759-1805): DIE
RÄUBER. 1: Manfred Karge –
Matthias Langhoff. 2-3: Pieter Hein.
5: Tilo Medek.
6: Volksbühne. Berlin D.D.R. 1971.
7: Maria Steinfeldt.

121

122

123

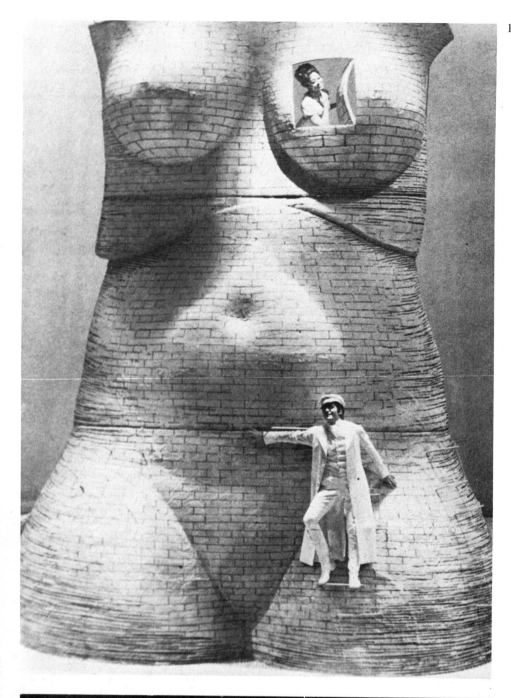

124 – ○ **– GIOACCHINO ROSSINI** (1792-1868): IL BARBIERE DI SIVIGLIA.
1: Ruth Berghaus. 2-3: Andreas Reinhardt. 5: Cesare Sterbini.
6: Bayerische Staatsoper. München (BRD). 1974.
7: Sabine Toepffer.

125 – □ **– ADAM MICKIEWICZ** (1798-1855): DZIADY.
1-2: Konrad Swinarski. 3: Krystyna Zachwatowicz. 4: Zofia Wieclawowna.
5: Zygmunt Konieczny.
6: Stary Teatr im. Heleny Modrzejewskiej. Krakow (Polska). 1973. 7: Wojciech Plewinski.

The traditional division between stage and house is gone.

Scène et salle s'interpénètrent.

126 – □ **– ALEXANDR POUSHKIN** (1799-1837): BORIS GODOUNOV.
1: Vladimir Ivanov.
2-3: Edouard Kotcherghine.
6: Pskovskij Oblastnoj Dramatitcheskij Teatr. Pskov (S.S.S.R.). 1973.
7: B. Stourabov.

The backdrop in made of hemp decorated with rags of all sorts : sack-cloth, winding sheets. In places the rags are held with old brocade, the kind which was once used in sacerdotal garments. Of the fifty bells utilized in the production, twenty-five are authentic and were borrowed from churches in Pskov. (Edouard Kotcherghine)

Le fond est tendu d'une toile de chanvre décorée de lambeaux de toutes sortes : toile de sac et toile d'emballage. Par endroits, ces lambeaux sont retenus par des applications de brocart ancien, celui qui servait pour les habits sacerdotaux. Sur les cinquante cloches que nous utilisons dans le spectacle, vingt-cinq sont authentiques et ont été empruntées à diverses églises de Pskov.
(Edouard Kotcherghine)

127

127/129 – □ – GEORG BÜCHNER
(1813-1837): DANTONS TOD.
1-2: Michael Meschke.
3: Françoise Grund. 5: Karl Erik
Welin. 6: Marionetteatern – Dramaten.
Stockholm. 1971. 7: Beata Bergström.

*The old Parliament building is
merely a realistic environment for a
non-theatrical confrontation of
ideas which creates intellectually
a revolutionary reality.
(Michael Meschke)*

Le spectacle se déroule dans les
bâtiments de l'ancien Parlement.
Environnement réaliste pour une
confrontation non-théâtrale d'opi-
nions qui, pour le moins, renvoient
à une réalité révolutionnaire.
(Michael Meschke)

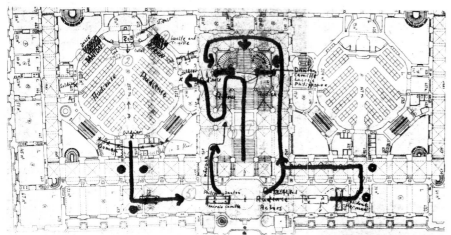

128

130 – □ – GEORG BÜCHNER
(1813-1837): LEONCE UND LENA.
1-2-3: Liviu Ciulei. 5: Theodor
Grigoriu. 6: Teatrul Lucia Sturdza
Bulandra. Bucuresti. 1970.
7: Clara Spitzer.

129

131 – ○ – RICHARD WAGNER
(1813-1883): DER RING DES
NIEBELUNGEN (DAS RHEIN-
GOLD). 1-2-3: Wolfgang Wagner.
6: Die Bayreuther Festspiele.
Bayreuth (BRD). 1970.
7: Festspiele Bayreuth.

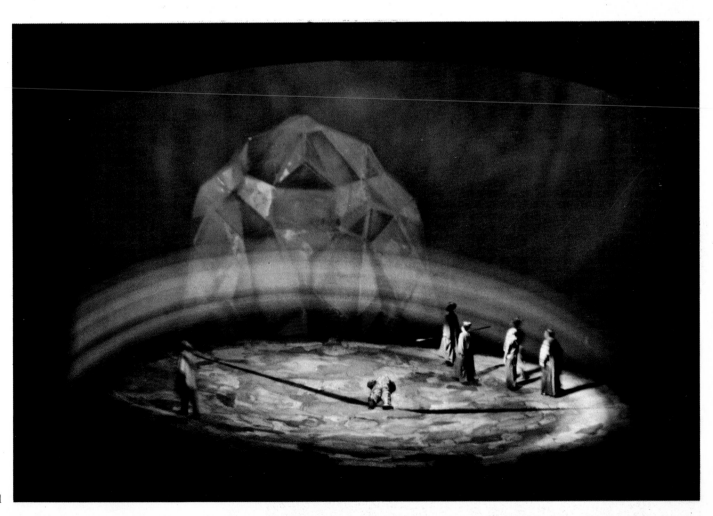

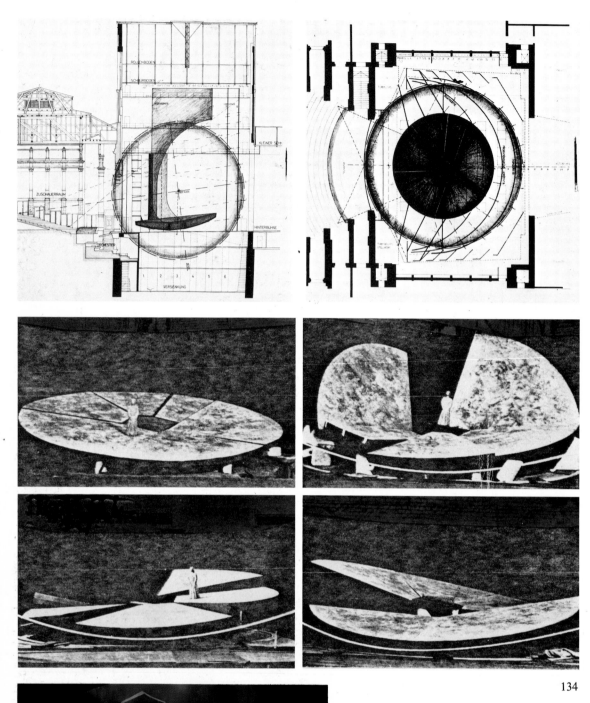

134

135

136

132/139 – ○ – RICHARD WAGNER (1813-1883): DER RING DES NIEBELUNGEN (DAS RHEINGOLD 135/136, DIE WALKÜRE 137, GÖTTERDÄMMERUNG 138/139). 1-2-3: Wolfgang Wagner. 6: Die Bayreuther Festspiele. Bayreuth (BRD). 1970. 7: Festspiele Bayreuth.

Formal and symbolic unity is provided by a large concave disc, an image of the ring and, one could say, of the cosmos... Intact in RHEINGOLD, this disc breaks into various fragments as the crimes accumulate. Its segments become, one after the other, mycenean blocks for the kingdom of Wotan; boulders floating between heaven and earth, home of the Valkyr; and the somber and sinister chaos in which Mime conceals his forge. Finally, in TWILIGHT OF THE GODS, after the cataclysmic and purifying events, the circle rediscovers its smooth and regular surface, evocative of a new world, a new departure...
(Jacques Mairel. Le Soir)

Unité formelle et symbolique à partir du grand disque concave, image de l'anneau, et, pourrait-on dire, du cosmos... Intact dans l'OR DU RHIN, ce disque se brise en différents fragments au fur et à mesure que s'accumulent les crimes; ses segments deviennent tour à tour blocs mycéniens du royaume de Wotan, rochers voguant entre ciel et terre, où évoluent les Walkyries, chaos sombre et sinistre où Mime a dissimulé sa forge; et nous savons que dans le CRÉPUSCULE, après les grands cataclysmes purificateurs, le cercle retrouvera sa surface lisse et régulière, évocatrice d'un nouveau monde, d'un nouveau départ...
(Jacques Mairel. Le Soir)

137

138

139

140

141

142

140/142 – ○ – GIUSEPPE VERDI
(1813-1901): LA TRAVIATA.
1: Maurice Béjart. 2-3: Thierry
Bosquet. 5: F.M. Piave.
6: Opéra National. Théâtre Royal de
la Monnaie. Bruxelles. 1974.

*Each of the four acts contains a
«coup de théâtre». The first one is
the antique gold decor, purple
hangings and chandeliers of the
auditorium of the Brussels Opera
House which remains on stage
throughout the opera.
In the third act, a giant roulette
wheel appears, to which the extras
in evening dress bring their gold bars.
(Olivier Merlin. Le Monde)*

Chacun des quatre actes comporte
un « coup de théâtre ». Le premier
de tous est la reconstitution sur la
scène du cadre vieil or à tentures
pourpres et à girandoles de la
Monnaie, qui restera planté pendant
tout l'opéra.
Au troisième acte le plateau figure
une roulette géante où des figurants
en habit apportent leurs lingots.
(Olivier Merlin. Le Monde)

**143/144 – □ – EUGENE
LABICHE** (1815-1888): LA
CAGNOTTE.
1: Peter Stein. 2: Karl-Ernst
Herrmann. 3: Susanne Raschig.
6: Schaubühne am Halleschen Ufer.
Berlin (West). 1973. 7: Ilse Buhs.

*The action unfolds in an avalanche,
like the jokes of an old silent movie.
Peter Stein is not interested in effects,
but in motives and causes. Those who
think they can buy the world with
one pot are swallowed up by big
money.*

L'action se déroule en avalanche,
comme les gags du film muet.
Peter Stein ne s'intéresse pas aux
effets, mais aux mobiles et aux
causes. Ceux qui croient pouvoir
acheter le monde avec une cagnotte
sont avalés par le gros capital.

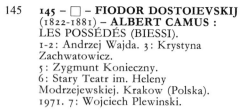

145 – □ – FIODOR DOSTOIEVSKIJ
(1822-1881) – **ALBERT CAMUS :**
LES POSSÉDÉS (BIESSI).
1-2: Andrzej Wajda. 3: Krystyna
Zachwatowicz.
5: Zygmunt Konieczny.
6: Stary Teatr im. Heleny
Modrzejewskiej. Krakow (Polska).
1971. 7: Wojciech Plewinski.

*It is the interrelationship of words
and gestures, of thoughts, images
and emotions which constitutes the
form of this production.*

C'est la correspondance des mots et
des gestes, des pensées, des
émotions et des images qui constitue
la forme de ce spectacle.

**146/147 – □ – FIODOR
DOSTOIEVSKIJ** (1822-1881) –
VICTOR ROZOV :
BRAT ALIOSHA (BRATIA
KARAMAZOV). 1: Adolf Shapiro.
2-3: Mark Kitaïev.
6: Teatr Younogo Zritelia. Riga
(S.S.S.R.). 1973.
7: Yourij Ikonnikov.

*At the very rear of the stage there is
a second smaller playing area which,
contains the settings specifying the
locale of each scene.
All the episodes begin there, but,
during the action, the characters
leave this specific place to play in a
conventional space where pure
dialogue is king.
(Adolf Shapiro)*

Tout au fond du plateau, une
seconde scène toute petite : c'est là
que se trouve ramassé le décor
situant le lieu. C'est là que com-
mencent la plupart des épisodes.
Au cours de l'action, les personnages
quittent cet endroit connu pour
gagner un espace conventionnel où
le dialogue est roi.
(Adolf Shapiro) .

**148/154 – □ – FIODOR
DOSTOIEVSKIJ** (1822-1881) –
PREDRAG BAJCETIC :
SLADOSTRASNICI KARAMAZOVI
(BRATIA KARAMAZOV).
1: Predrag Bajcetic. 2: Slobodan Masic.
3: Bozana Jovanovic. 5: Zoran Hristic.
6: Atelje 212. Beograd. 1974.
7: Vladimir Blagojevic.

148

149

150

155

156

157

158/160

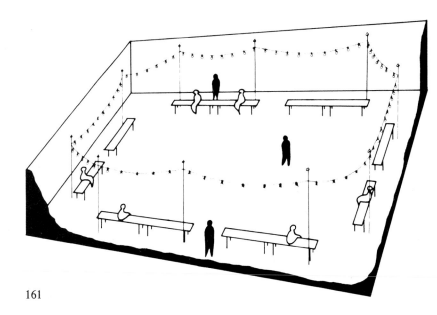

161

155/162 – ☐ – FIODOR DOSTOIEVSKIJ (1822-1881) –
EUGENIO BARBA : MIN FARS
HUS. 1: Eugenio Barba.
2-3: Odin Teatret. 6: Odin Teatret.
Holstebro (Danmark). 1972.
7: Tony d'Urso (155/157) –
Odin Teatret (158/160) – Roald Pay
(162).

*The production results from an
encounter between Dostoevsky and us.
Allusions to his life and his books
are visible, but all has been seen
through the filter of what we are,
our experiences and our longings.
A reconnaissance mission in the
House of the Father.
(Eugenio Barba)*

Le spectacle est le résultat de la
rencontre entre Dostoievski et nous.
On peut y discerner des allusions à
sa vie et à ses œuvres, mais tout a
passé par le filtre de nos vérités,
expériences et nostalgies. Un tour de
reconnaissance dans la Maison du
Père.
(Eugenio Barba)

162

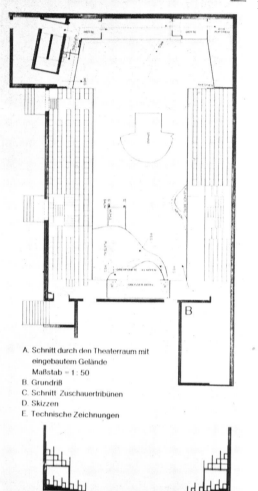

A. Schnitt durch den Theaterraum mit
   eingebautem Gelände
   Maßstab = 1 : 50
B. Grundriß
C. Schnitt Zuschauertribünen
D. Skizzen
E. Technische Zeichnungen

164

165

163/168 – ⬜ – HENRIK IBSEN
(1828-1906): PEER GYNT.
1: Peter Stein. 2: Karl-Ernst Herrmann.
3: M. Bickel – J. Herzog –
S. Raschig. 5: Peter Fischer.
6: Schaubühne am Halleschen Ufer.
Berlin (West). 1971. 7: Ilse Buhs.

*The scenic space of PEER GYNT is
made up of three zones : a large
intermediary space where Peer can
play out his imaginary self and,
on each side, two platform stages,
both proscenium spaces, one for
various events like the theft of the
boat, the other where Solveig waits
for Peer.
(Peter Stein)*

...L'espace scénique de PEER GYNT
est composé de trois zones : un
large espace intermédiaire où Peer
Gynt peut déployer son moi imaginaire et, des deux côtés de cet
espace, deux estrades qui font
fonction de scènes à l'italienne,
l'une où se produisent divers
événements, comme le vol du
bateau, l'autre où Solveig attend
Gynt.
(Peter Stein)

166

*PEER GYNT doesn't belong to the
theatre of illusion. It describes an
illusion.*

PEER GYNT n'appartient pas au
théâtre de l'illusion : il décrit une
illusion.

167

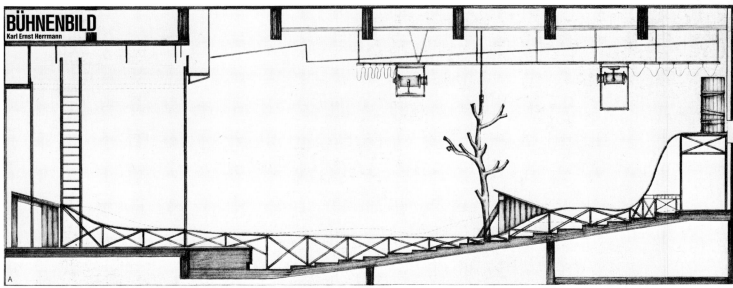

168

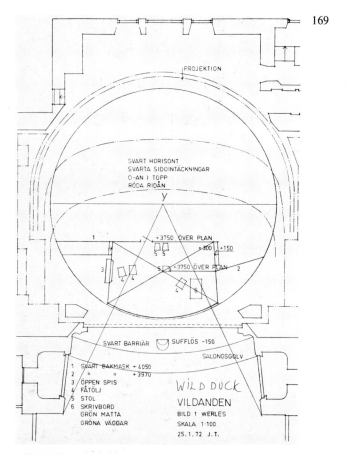

SVART HORISONT
SVARTA SIDOINTÄCKNINGAR
0-AN I TOPP
RÖDA RIDÅN

PROJEKTION

+3750 ÖVER PLAN

+3750 ÖVER PLAN

SVART BARRIÄR   SUFFLÖS -150

SALONGSGOLV

1 SVART BAKMASK +4050
2 "   "   +3970
3 ÖPPEN SPIS
4 FÅTÖLJ
5 STOL
6 SKRIVBORD
GRÖN MATTA
GRÖNA VÄGGAR

WILD DUCK

VILDANDEN
BILD 1 WERLES
SKALA 1:100
25.1.72 J.T.

169/173 – □ – HENRIK IBSEN
(1828-1906): VILDANDEN.
1: Ingmar Bergman. 2: Marik Vos.
6: Dramatiska Teatern. Stockholm.
1972. 7: Beata Bergström.

It is around Hedvig's death – that meaningless sacrifice provoked by Gregers Werle, the champion of truth – that Bergman's production is concentrated and attains its truest moment.

C'est autour de la mort d'Hedvig – sacrifice inutile que provoque Gregers Werle, le pourfendeur de mensonges – que tourne la mise en scène de Bergman et qu'elle atteint sa plus grande vérité.

174

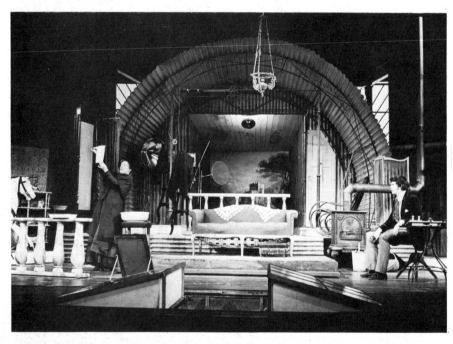

175

176

174/176 – □ – HENRIK IBSEN
(1828-1906): VILDANDEN.
1: Manfred Karge – Matthias Langhoff.
2-3: Dieter Hein.
6: Volksbühne. Berlin D.D.R. 1973.
7: Maria Steinfeldt.

Karge and Langhoff show how and why Ibsen's world is piteously funny.
(Eric De Kuyper. Clés)

Karge et Langhoff montrent et démontrent en quoi et par quoi le monde d'Ibsen est pitoyablement drôle.
(Eric De Kuyper. Clés)

177

177/178 – □ – ALEKSIS KIVI
(1834-1872): SEITSEMÄN
VELJESTÄ. 1: Kalle Holmberg.
2: Kaj Puumalainen. 3: Mans Hedström.
5: Kaj Chydenius. 6: Turun
Kaupunginteatteri. Turku (Suomi).
1972. 7: Klaus Koszubatis.

The cornerstone of Finnish epic...
Civilization has no hold on the seven brothers. But they will be separated, their farm demolished, and a new chapter will unfold in the history of Finnish agriculture.
(Kalle Holmberg)

La pierre angulaire de l'épopée finlandaise... La civilisation n'a pas de prise sur les sept frères; mais on arrivera à dissoudre leur groupe, leur ferme sera démolie et un nouveau chapitre s'ouvrira dans l'histoire de l'agriculture finlandaise.
(Kalle Holmberg)

178

179 – □ – ION CREANGA
(1839-1889): HARAP ALB.
1: Zoe Anghel Stanca.
2: Vladimir Popov. 3: Diana Ioan
Popov. 4: Gheorghe Caciuleanu.
5: Lucian Ionescu.
6: Teatrul Tineretului. Piatra Neamt
(Romania). 1970. 7: Scînteii.

All the scenic elements are mobile and change in the light : the stage moves from white to colored light, to end with the black light of quartz lamps.

Tous les éléments scénographiques sont mobiles et jouent dans la lumière : on passe du blanc aux lumières colorées, pour finir avec la lumière noire des quartz.

179

180

The appropriate set of furniture and actors are brought together from time to time according to the sequence of the story. At such moments, the bars are moved wider apart, thus allowing better visibility of the actors.

Le mobilier adéquat et les acteurs sont mis en place séquence par séquence. Alors les barres de la cage s'écartent pour permettre une meilleure visibilité.

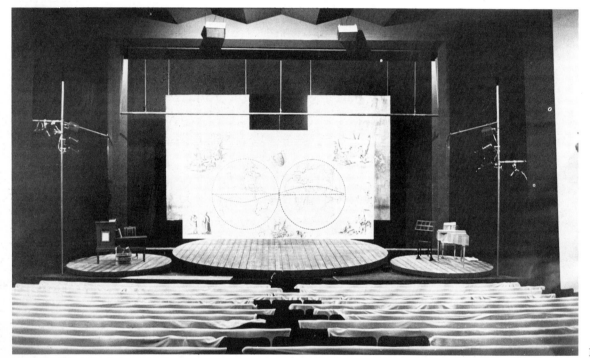

181

Ruthlessy and wilfully, in the manner of Strindberg, Bergman shows the oppositions between semblance and reality. The conservative society reproduces itself according to the eternal law of repetition.

Sans repos ni merci, dans la ligne de Strindberg, Bergman montre les contradictions entre apparence et réalité. La société conservatrice se reproduit selon l'éternelle loi de répétition.

182

184

185

186

184 – ☐ – ANTON TCHEKHOV
(1860-1904): DIADIA VANIA.
1: Erwin Axer. 2-3: Eva Starowieyska.
5: Michael Rüggeberg.
6: Münchner Kammerspiele.
München (BRD). 1972.
7: Hildegard Steinmetz.

185 – ☐ – ANTON TCHEKHOV
(1860-1904): DIADIA VANIA.
1: Otto Homlung.
2-3: Christian Egemar.
6: Den Nationale Scene. Lille Scene.
Bergen (Norge). 1971.
7: Trygve Schönfelder.

186 – ☐○ – SEVERINO REYES
(1861-1942) – **FULGENCIO**
TOLENTINO :
WALANG SUGAT.
1: Daisy H. Avellana. 2: Lamberto
V. Avellana. 3. Pedrito Legaspi.
4: Joji Felix-Velarde. 6: Zarzuella
Foundation of the Philippines. The
Cultural Center of the Philippines
Theatre. Manila. 1971.
7: Nath Gutierrez.

After the American occupation of the
Philippines, a group of Filipinos set
out to write inflammatory propa-
ganda plays masquerading as
Zarzuelas...

Après l'occupation des Philippines
par les Américains, un groupe de
Filipinos se mit à écrire des pièces
de propagande incendiaire
camouflées en Zarzuelas...

187/188 – ☐ – ARTHUR
SCHNITZLER (1862-1931):
LIEBELEI. 1: Hans Hollmann.
2-3: Wolfgang Mai.
6: Komödie. Basel (Helvetia). 1973.
7: Peter Stöckli.

Hollmann disjointed the play by,
on the one hand, making the actors
play in a distanced way; on the
other hand, he reintroduced sentimen-
tal and almost literal lyricism by
having a pianist and violinist
accompany the play.
(Eric De Kuyper. Clés)

Hollmann a désarticulé la pièce en
faisant jouer, d'une part, aux
comédiens le texte d'une façon
détachée; d'autre part, il a réintro-
duit un lyrisme sentimental
presque littéral en faisant accom-
pagner la pièce par deux musiciens,
un pianiste et un violoniste.
(Eric De Kuyper. Clés)

187

188

189

190

189/190 – ☐ – **ARTHUR SCHNITZLER** (1862-1931): LIEBELEI. 1: Gerhard Klingenberg. 2-3: Rouben Ter-Arutunian. 6: Akademietheater. Wien. 1972. 7: Elisabeth Hausmann.

191 – ☐ – **FRANK WEDEKIND** (1864-1918): DER MARQUIS VON KEITH. 1: Dieter Giesing. 2-3: Jürgen Rose. 6: Münchner Kammerspiele. München (BRD). 1970. 7: Hildegard Steinmetz.

192 – ☐ – **FRANK WEDEKIND** (1864-1918): SCHLOSZ WETTERSTEIN. 1: Arno Wustenhofer. 2: Wilfried Minks. 3: Wilfried Minks – Rolf Glittenberg. 5: Klaus Melchers. 6: Wuppertaler Bühnen. Wuppertal (BRD). 1972. 7: Ilse Buhs.

The central theme is the elemental force of sex and its antagonism to a conventional society.

La puissance élémentaire du sexe opposée aux conventions de la société.

193 – ☐ – **HERMAN HEIJERMANS**
(1864-1924): SCHAKELS.
1: Wim van Rooij. 2-3: Harry Wich.
6: De Haagse Comedie. Koninklijke
Schouwburg. Den Haag (Nederland).
1971. 7: Pan Sok.

194 – ☐ – **RAMON MARIA DEL
VALLE-INCLAN** (1866-1936):
LA MARQUESA ROSALINDA.
1: Miguel Narros. 2: Francisco Nieva.
5: Manuel Angulo. 6: Teatro Español.
Madrid. 1970. 7: Manuel Martinez
Muñoz.

195/198 – □ – LUIGI PIRANDELLO
(1867-1936): COSI E SE VI PARE.
1: Giorgio De Lullo. 2-3: Pier Luigi
Pizzi. 6: Compagnia De Lullo – Falk –
Valli – Albani. Teatro Valle. Roma.
1972. 7: Tommaso Le Pera.

Pier Luigi Pizzi turned his back on
the traditional 1927 Roman villa :
he built, on the pretext of creating
a refined bourgeois interior, scenic
spaces which, by their very structure,
suggest Mies van der Rohe and the
Bauhaus.
(Mario Raimondo. Il Dramma)

Pier Luigi Pizzi a tourné le dos à la
petite villa romaine style 1927 :
il a bâti, sur la fiction d'un intérieur
bourgeois raffiné, des lieux scéni-
ques qui , par leur structure, peuvent
évoquer Mies van der Rohe et le
Bauhaus.
(Mario Raimondo. Il Dramma)

195 / 197

198

199 – □ – MAXIM GORKIJ
(1868-1936): DIETI SOLNTSA.
1: Jan Kacer. 2: Jozef Svoboda.
3: Jindriska Hirschova.
5: Zdenek Pololanik.
6: Narodni divadlo. Praha. 1973.
7: Jaromir Svoboda.

201

200 – □ – EDMOND ROSTAND
(1868-1918): CYRANO DE
BERGERAC. 1: Miroslav Machacek.
2: Jozef Svoboda. 3: Jarmila Konecna.
4: Ivan Chrz. 5: Miroslav Ponc.
6: Narodni divadlo. Praha. 1974.
7: Jaromir Svoboda.

**201 – □ – STANISLAW
WYSPIANSKI** (1869-1907):
WYZWOLENIE.
1: Konrad Swinarski.
2-3: Kazimierz Wisniak.
5: Zygmunt Konieczny.
6: Stary Teatr im. Heleny
Modrzejewskiej. Krakow (Polska).
1974. 7: Wojciech Plewinski.

202

**202 – □ – JOHN MILLINGTON
SYNGE** (1871-1909):
THE TINKER'S WEDDING.
1: Dieter Berner. 2: Ambrosius Humm.
3: Renate Kalanke. 5: Pepe Solbach.
6: Theater am Neumarkt. Zürich
(Helvetia). 1974. 7: Leonard Zubler.

203 – □ – ROBERT WALSER
(1872-1957): ALLE GEHEN GEGEN
DAS SCHLOSZ.
1: Jan Grossmann.
2-3: Ambrosius Humm.
5: Zdenek Sikola.
6: Theater am Neumarkt. Zürich
(Helvetia). 1972. 7: Leonard Zubler.

203

204

204 – ☐ – ALFRED JARRY (1873-1907): UBU-ROI.
1: Shmuel Bunim. 2-3: Ruth Dar.
6. Teatron Ha-Cameri. Tel-Aviv. 1971.
7: Mula – Haramaty.

205/208 – ○ – ARNOLD SCHÖNBERG (1874-1951): MOSES UND ARON.
1: Götz Friedrich. 2-3: Rudolf Heinrich.
4: Erich Walter. 6: Staatsoper. Wien.
1973. 7: Elisabeth Hausmann.

209 – ☐ – SEM BENELLI (1877-1949): LA CENA DELLE BEFFE.
1-2-3: Carmelo Bene. 5: Vittorio Gelmetti. 6: Teatro Stabile dell'Aquila. L'Aquila (Italia). 1973.
7: Pietro Pascuttini.

I see the JEST as the story of an athletic victory...
(Carmelo Bene)

La CENA, je la vois comme l'histoire d'une victoire sportive.
(Carmelo Bene)

210 – ☐ – ANDRIS OUPITE (1877-1970): JEANNA D'ARC.
1: Arkadij Katz. 2: Ilmar Bloumberg. 3: Andris Freiberg,
5: Paul Dajbis.
6: Rousskij Dramatitcheskij Teatr. Riga (S.S.S.R.). 1972.
7: Yourij Ikonnikov.

The plastic conception reflects the development of the play. From the white of nothingness to black. From the emptiness of space to the concentration of everyday objects which shall form the pyre.
(Ilmar Bloumberg)

La conception plastique reflète l'évolution de la pièce. Du néant blanc au noir. De l'espace vide à la concentration d'objets usuels qui vont former le bûcher.
(Ilmar Bloumberg)

205/208

209

210

211

211/213 – □ – **CARL STERNHEIM**
(1878-1942): DIE HOSE – DER
SNOB – 1913 (IL CICLO
DELL'EROE BORGHESE).
1: Mario Missiroli. 2: Giancarlo
Bignardi. 3: Elena Mannini.
6: Compagnia Teatro Opera Due.
Teatro delle Arti. Roma. 1973.
7: Marcello Norberth.

212

214 – □ – **FRANZ KAFKA** (1883-
1924) – **JERZY GRZEGORZEWSKI**:
AMERIKA.
1-2-3: Jerzy Grzegorzewski.
5: Stanislaw Radwan.
6: Teatr Ateneum. Warszawa. 1973.
7: Edward Hartwig.

*The action is played in the lobby
and the check-room of the theatre.*

L'action est jouée dans le vestiaire
et le hall du théâtre.

213

215 – □ – **STANISLAW IGNACY
WITKIEWICZ** (1885-1939):
METAFIZYKA DWUGLOWEGO
CIELECIA. 1: Richard Vachoux.
2-3: Jean Monod.
6: Nouveau Théâtre de Poche.
Genève (Helvetia). 1971.
7: Jacques Bétant.

216

217 218

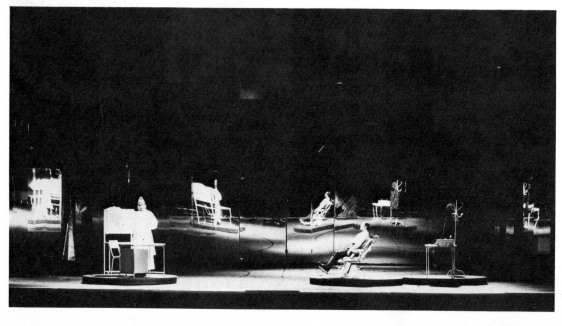

219

216/219 – ◯ – **ALBAN BERG**
(1885-1935): WOZZECK.
1: Karel Jernek. 2: Jozef Svoboda.
5: Alban Berg – Georg Büchner.
6: Teatro alla Scala. Milano (Italia).
1971. 7: Ezio Piccagliani.

220

221

220/221 – ▢ – **EUGENE O'NEILL**
(1888-1953): STRANGE
INTERLUDE.
1: Giancarlo Sbragia. 2-3: Vittorio
Rossi. 5: Giancarlo Sbragia.
6: Gli Associati. Teatro Verdi.
Padova (Italia). 1972. 7: Team.

222

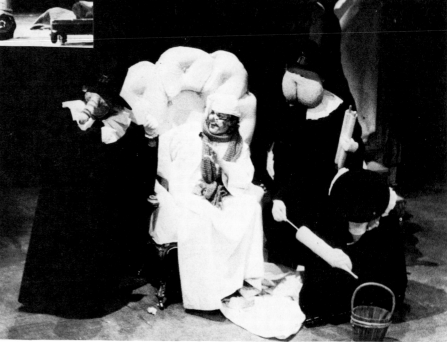

223

224

222/223 – ☐ – MIKHAIL BOULGAKOV (1891-1940) –
MOLIÈRE – LUIGI SQUARZINA :
MOLIER (IL TARTUFFO OVVERO
VITA, AMORI, AUTOCENSURA E
MORTE IN SCENA DEL SIGNOR
DI MOLIÈRE, NOSTRO
CONTEMPORANEO).
1 : Luigi Squarzina. 2-3 : Gianfranco
Padovani. 5 : Fernando Cs Mainardi.
6 : Teatro Stabile di Genova. Genova
(Italia). 1971. 7 : Publifoto.

For this production, I combined two
texts, MOLIER by Bulgakov and
Molière's TARTUFFE.
Molière provides a classical perspective
to the autobiographical tragi-comedy
of Bulgakov.
(Luigi Squarzina)

J'ai combiné deux textes : le
MOLIÈRE de Boulgakov et le
TARTUFFE de Molière. Molière
donne un souffle classique à la
tragi-comédie autobiographique de
Boulgakov.
(Luigi Squarzina)

225

**224 – ◯ – SERGHEJ
PROKOFIEV** (1891-1952):
SEMION KOTKO.
1 : Boris Pokrovskij. 2-3 : Valerij
Levental. 4 : Boris Pokrovskij.
5 : Valentine Kataïev.
6 : Gossoudarstvennyj
Akademitcheskij Bolshoj Teatr
Soyouza SSR. Moskva. 1970.

226

225/227 – ◯ – PAUL DESSAU (1894):
EINSTEIN.
1 : Ruth Berghaus. 2-3 : Andreas
Reinhardt. 5 : Karl Mickel.
6 : Deutsche Staatsoper. Berlin D.D.R.
1974. 7 : Maria Steinfeldt.

The moral dilemma of the XXth
century scientist. Einstein's life
from his expulsion from Germany
to the atomic bomb.

La problématique de l'homme de
science au XXᵉ siècle. Au fil des
étapes de la vie d'Einstein depuis
son expulsion d'Allemagne jusqu'à
la bombe atomique.

227

228

228 – □ – BERTOLT BRECHT
(1898-1956): BAAL.
1: François Rochaix.
2-3: Jean-Claude Maret.
6: Atelier de Genève – Théâtre de
Carouge. Festival du Jeune Théâtre.
Maison de la Culture des Chiroux.
Liège (Belgique). 1972.
7: Daniel Vittet.

1 salle de réception - 2 noce
3 table aux cadeaux - 4 salle
à manger - 5 public - 6 table
de noce - 7 piano - 8 armoire
9 sofa - 10 étagère

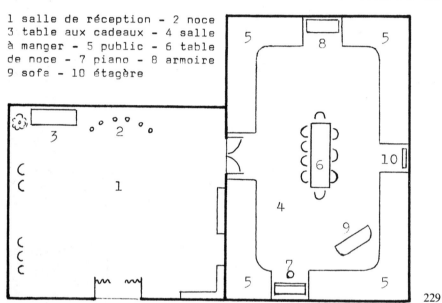

229

229/230 – □ – BERTOLT BRECHT
(1898-1956): DIE KLEINBÜRGER-
HOCHZEIT. 1: Jaak Vissenaken.
2: Robert Seyffer. 6: Centrum voor
Theaterstudio. Brugge (België). 1971.

*The production begins outside, then
the spectator participates in the
toasts and congratulates the young
marrieds...*

Le spectacle commence à l'extérieur.
Ensuite, le spectateur participe au
vin d'honneur et félicite les jeunes
mariés...

230

**231/232 – □ – BERTOLT
BRECHT** (1898-1956): DIE
DREIGROSCHENOPER.
1: Giorgio Strehler. 2-3: Ezio Frigerio.
4: Marise Flach. 5: Kurt Weill.
6: Piccolo Teatro di Milano.
Teatro Metastasio. Prato (Italia). 1973.
7: Luigi Ciminaghi (231) – Team (232).

231

232

233/237 – ☐ – **BERTOLT BRECHT**
(1898-1956): DIE HEILIGE
JOHANNA DER SCHLACHT-
HÖFE. 1: Eugen Terttula. 2-3: Dan
Nemteanu. 5: Ilkka Kuusisto.
6: Helsingin Kaupunginteatteri.
Helsinki. 1972. 7: Kari Hakli.

235

237

236

239

238 – □○ – **BERTOLT BRECHT**
(1898-1956) – **KURT WEILL :**
DIE SIEBEN TODSÜNDEN.
1 : Gene Sagan. 2 : Dani Karavan.
4 : Gene Sagan. 6 : Ha-Ensemble
Ha-Cameri Haysraeli. Israël. 1972.
7 : Jaacov Agor.

239 – □ – **BERTOLT BRECHT**
(1898-1956): DIE AUSNAHME
UND DIE REGEL.
1 : Sam Walters. 2 : Richard
Montgomery. 6 : Little Theatre.
Kingston (Jamaica – West Indies).
1970. 7 : Richard Montgomery.

240

240 – □ – **BERTOLT BRECHT**
(1898-1956): MUTTER COURAGE.
1 : Antoine Vitez. 2 : Yannis Kokkos.
3 : Danièle Rozier. 5 : Paul Dessau.
6 : Théâtre des Quartiers d'Ivry –
Théâtre des Amandiers. Nanterre
(France). 1973.

*The stage represents a road : the
road which Courage perpetually
travels with her wagon, a baby-
carriage.*
(Antoine Vitez)

**La scène représente un chemin :
le chemin que parcourt perpétuel-
lement Courage avec sa voiture –
une voiture d'enfant.
(Antoine Vitez)**

241/242 – □ – BERTOLT BRECHT
(1898-1956): DER GUTE MENSCH
VON SEZUAN. 1: Benno Besson.
2-3: Achim Freyer. 5: Paul Dessau.
6: Volksbühne. Berlin D.D.R. 1970.
7: Harry Hirschfeld.

241

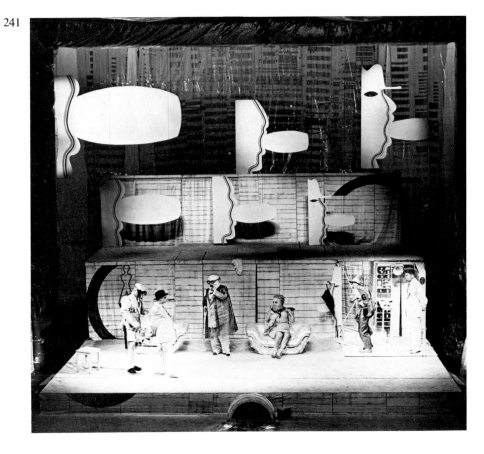

242

243

244

245

246

247

243/247 – □ – BERTOLT BRECHT
(1898-1956): TURANDOT ODER
DER KONGRESZ DER
WEISZWÄSCHER.
1: Peter Kupke – Wolfgang Pintzka.
2: Karl Von Appen. 3: Eberhard
Keienburg. 5: Hans-Dieter Hosalla.
6: Berliner Ensemble. Berlin D.D.R.
1973. 7: Vera Tenschert (243) – Maria
Steinfeldt (244/246) – Percy Paukschta
(247).

*Cotton has become rare in the
Chinese Empire. Where has it gone?
No one dares answer : to the ware-
houses of the Emperor who hoards it
in order to raise the prices. The
hand of Princess Turandot will go
to whomever can furnish an acceptable
reply.*

Dans l'Empire de Chine, le coton
est devenu rare. Où a-t-il disparu ?
Personne n'ose répondre : dans les
greniers de l'Empereur qui thésau-
rise le coton pour faire monter les
prix. Qui fournira une réponse
acceptable obtiendra la main de la
princesse Turandot.

248/249 – ☐ – FEDERICO GARCIA LORCA (1898-1936): YERMA.
1: Victor Garcia. 2-3: Victor Garcia – Fabian Puigserver. 6: Compañia Nuria Espert. Théâtre de la Ville. Paris. 1973. 7: Michel Berger.

YERMA is the play of frustration. Those who like it feel it symbolises the frustration of a country, those who don't say it's only about a frustrated woman.
(Nuria Espert)

C'est la pièce de la frustration. Ceux qui l'aiment pensent qu'elle symbolise la frustration d'un pays. Ceux qui ne l'aiment pas, qu'il s'agit simplement d'une femme frustrée.
(Nuria Espert)

248

249

It was played on a gigantic trampoline which suggested, in turn, a Granada mountainside, the sail of a ship seen in Yerma's nightmare, a living womb and a beating heart.
(Eric Johns. Theatre Reviews 1973)

YERMA se joue sur un gigantesque trampoline, qui suggère tour à tour les montagnes de Grenade, la voile d'un bateau aperçue dans le cauchemar de Yerma, un ventre de femme et un cœur battant.
(Eric Johns. Theatre Reviews 1973)

250/251 – □ – FEDERICO GARCIA LORCA (1898-1936): YERMA.
1: Franz Marijnen. 2-3: Andrei Ivaneanu-Damaschin. 5: Koen De Kouter. 6: Nederlands Toneel Gent. Gent (België). 1973.
7: Juul Vandevelde.

For Franz Marijnen, this play is less about sterility than the destruction of social taboos, norms and structures. The liberation of women is its essential element.

Pour Franz Marijnen, ce drame est moins celui de la stérilité que de la destruction des tabous sociaux, des normes et des structures; la libération de la femme en est l'élément essentiel.

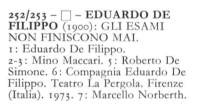

252/253 – □ – EDUARDO DE FILIPPO (1900): GLI ESAMI NON FINISCONO MAI.
1: Eduardo De Filippo.
2-3: Mino Maccari. 5: Roberto De Simone. 6: Compagnia Eduardo De Filippo. Teatro La Pergola. Firenze (Italia). 1973. 7: Marcello Norberth.

254/255 – □ – MARIELUISE FLEISSER (1901-1974):
FEGEFEUER IN INGOLSTADT.
1: Peter Stein. 2: Karl-Ernst Herrmann.
3: Moidele Bickel.
6: Schaubühne am Halleschen Ufer.
Berlin (West). 1972.
7: Ilse Buhs.

A play about religious and adolescent delusions.
Marieluise Fleisser had been promoted by Brecht in the early thirties but she was only «discovered» during the sixties.

Une pièce sur les phantasmes religieux et les illusions adolescentes. Marieluise Fleisser, appréciée par Brecht dans les années 30, n'a été « découverte » qu'après 1960.

256/257 – □ – ÖDÖN VON HORVATH (1901-1938): GESCHICHTEN AUS DEM WIENER WALD.
1: Klaus Michael Gruber.
2: Karl-Ernst Herrmann.
3: Moidele Bickel.
6: Schaubühne am Halleschen Ufer.
Berlin (West). 1972. 7: Ilse Buhs.

An anti-sentimental view of Vienna after the First World War.

Une vue anti-sentimentale de Vienne après la Première Guerre Mondiale.

258 – □ – SAMUEL BECKETT (1906): EN ATTENDANT GODOT.
1: Otomar Krejca. 2: Josef Svoboda.
6: Salzburger Festspiele. Landestheater. Salzburg (Österreich). 1970.

259

260

261

259/260 – □ – **ALEXEI ARBOUZOV**
(1908): GOROD NA ZARÉ.
1: Adolf Shapiro. 2-3: Mark Kitaïev.
6: Teatr Younogo Zritelia.
Riga (S.S.S.R.). 1970.

262

261 – □ – **BOGDAN CIPLIC** (1910):
SLATKO PRAVOSLAVLJE.
1: Dimitrije Djurkovic. 2-3: Dusan
Ristic. 5: Zoran Hristic.
6: Atelje 212. Beograd. 1970.
7: Dragoljub Tosic.

263

262/264 – □ – **JEAN GENET** (1910):
LE BALCON. 1-2: Victor Garcia.
6: Teatro Ruth Escobar. São Paulo
(Brasil). 1970.

264

265

266

265/266 – □ – **DIEGO FABBRI**
(1911) – **DAVIDE LAJOLO :**
IL VIZIO ASSURDO.
1: Giancarlo Sbragia.
2-3: Gianni Polidori. 5: Alban Berg.
6: Gli Associati. Teatro Verdi.
Padova (Italia). 1974.
7: Gianni Polidori.

267

267 – □ – **EUGENE IONESCO**
(1912): MACBETT.
1-2: Liviu Ciulei.
3: Radu Boruzescu– Miruna
Boruzescu. 4: Heino Hallhuber.
5: Michael Rüggeberg.
6: Münchner Kammerspiele.
München (BRD). 1973.
7. Hildegard Steinmetz.

268

269

268/270 – □ – EUGENE IONESCO
(1912): JEUX DE MASSACRE.
1 : Henryk Tomaszewski.
2-3 : Kazimierz Wisniak.
5 : Zbigniew Karnecki.
6 : Teatr im. E. Wiercinskiego.
Wroclaw (Polska). 1973.
7 : Grazyna Wyszomirska.

*Henryk Tomaszewski has introduced
a supplementary character into
Ionesco's play : Death herself,
dancing, mocking and clowning in
the style of the fairground.*

**Henryk Tomaszewski a introduit,
dans la pièce de Ionesco, un per-
sonnage supplémentaire : la mort
elle-même dansante et moqueuse;
elle bouffonne dans le style de la
foire.**

270

271

271 – △ – **ALWIN NIKOLAIS**
(1912): TEMPLE.
2-3-4: Alwin Nikolais.
6: Alwin Nikolais Dance Theatre.
Théâtre de la Ville. Paris. 1974.
7: Michel Berger.

*Optical, electronic, cinetic art.
We forget as we follow these leotards
streaked with bright colors and
furrowed with shadows, that they
hide bodies, that they are the
extensions of masked faces.*
(Claude Sarraute. Le Monde)

Art optique, électronique, cinétique.
On oublie, à suivre ces maillots
creusés de trous d'ombre, rayés de
couleurs vives, qu'ils recouvrent des
membres, qu'ils prolongent des
visages au demeurant masqués.
(Claude Sarraute. Le Monde)

272

272/273 – △ – **ALWIN NIKOLAIS**
(1912): CROSS-FADE.
2-3-4: Alwin Nikolais.
6: Alwin Nikolais Dance Theatre.
Lyceum Theatre. New York (U.S.A.).
1974. 7: Michel Berger.

*...kaleidescopic projections metamor-
phose the protagonists into upsetting
muses or cross-hatched Chirico
models.*
(Olivier Merlin. Le Monde)

...les projections en kaléidoscope
métamorphosent les protagonistes
en muses inquiétantes ou en
mannequins vermiculés de Chirico.
(Olivier Merlin. Le Monde)

273

274/275 – △ – **ALWIN NIKOLAIS**
(1912): TRIPLE DUO.
2-3-4: Alwin Nikolais.
6: Alwin Nikolais Dance Theatre.
Théâtre de la Ville. Paris. 1974.
7: Michel Berger.

*Two couples camouflaged under
ponchos reproduce the significant
postures of a naked couple.*
(Olivier Merlin. Le Monde)

Deux couples camouflés sous des
ponchos reproduisent les attitudes
lisibles d'un couple nu.
(Olivier Merlin. Le Monde)

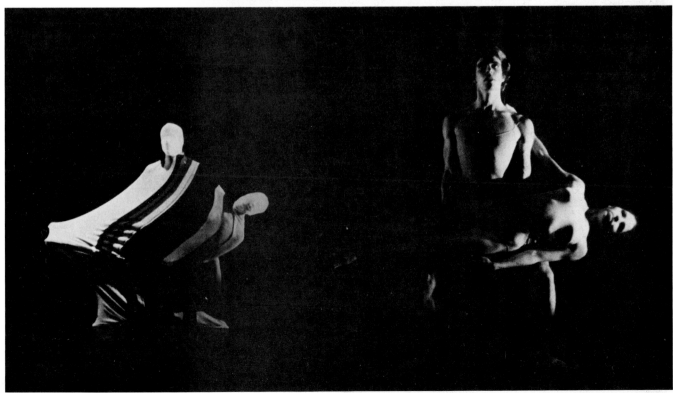

276 – □ – ISTVAN ÖRKÉNY (1912)
– ISTVAN NEMESKÜRTY :
A HOLTAK HALLGATASA.
1 : Zoltan Varkonyi. 2 : Miklos Feher.
6 : Vigszinhaz. Budapest. 1973. 7 : MTI.

After the battle of Stalingrad, the
2nd Hungarian Army had 100,000
dead. The play is a mosaic of
documents and memories.

Après la bataille de Stalingrad, la
IIème armée hongroise compte
100.000 morts. La pièce est une
mosaïque de documents et de
souvenirs.

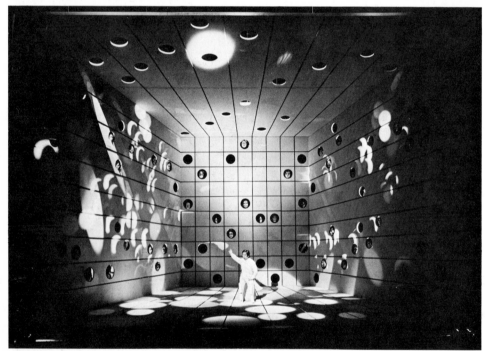

277 – □○ – TAIJUN TAKEDA
(1912) **– IKUMA DAN :**
HIKÁRIGOKE.
1 : Keita Asari. 2-3 : Kaoru Kanamori.
6 : Gékidan – Shiki. Nissei Gekijô.
Tokyo. 1973. 7 : Shigéko Higuchi.

The ceiling and the walls have
circular holes through which the
performers look out to sing their
parts.

Dans le plafond et les murs, des
ouvertures circulaires à travers
lesquelles chantent les interprètes.

278 – □ – VIKTORAS MILIUNAS
(1916) : KARUSÉLÉ.
1 : Vacys Blédis. 2-3 : Vytautas
Kalinauskas. 5 : Vytautas Barkauskas.
6 : Dramos Teatras. Panevezys
(S.S.S.R.). 1971.
7 : Eduardas Korizna.

279/280 – □ – PETER WEISS (1916) :
HÖLDERLIN.
1 : Claus Peymann. 2-3 : Adolf Steiof.
5 : Peer Raben.
6 : Deutsches Schauspielhaus.
Hamburg (BRD). 1971.
7 : Rosemarie Clausen.

281 – □ – PETER WEISS (1916) :
HÖLDERLIN.
1 : Peter Palitzsch. 2-3 : Karl Kneidl.
6 : Staatstheater. Stuttgart (BRD). 1971.
7 : Madeline Winkler-Betzendahl.

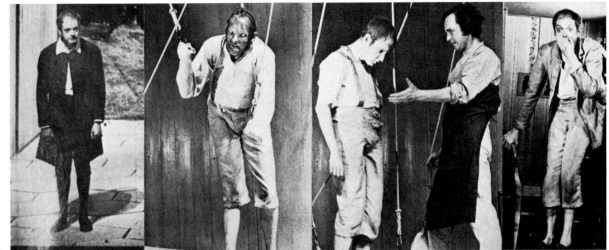

279

280

281

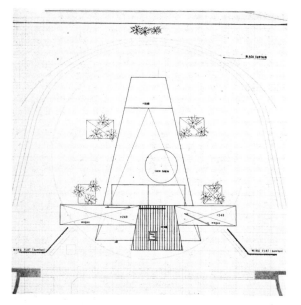
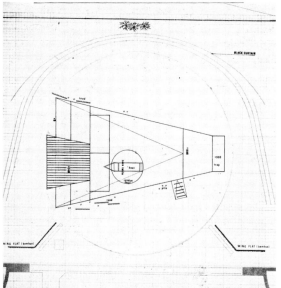

282/285 – □ – TSUTOMU MINAKAMI (1919): ECHIZEN TAKE NINGYO.
1: Koïchi Kimura. 2-3: Setsu Asakura. 5: Teizô Matsumura. 6: Gogatsu-sha. Kokuritsu Gekijô. Tokyo. 1973. 7: Shigéko Higuchi.

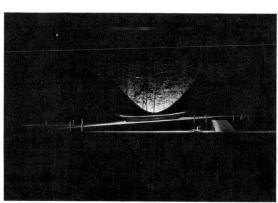

286 – □ – TADEUSZ ROZEWICZ (1921): NA CZWORAKACH.
1: Jerzy Jarocki. 2-3: Kazimierz Wisniak. 4: Jerzy Makarowski 5: Stanislaw Radwan. 6: Teatr Dramatyczny. Warszawa. 1972. 7: Renard Dudley.

A tragi-comedy. The writer Laurenty, classified by a label, rebels by clowning.

Une tragi-comédie. L'écrivain Laurenty, classé de son vivant sous une étiquette, se révolte en bouffonnant.

287 – □ – GIOVANNI TESTORI (1921): L'AMBLETO.
1: Franco Parenti. 2-3: Gian Maurizio Fercioni. 5: Fiorenzo Carpi. 6: Compagnia Teatro Franco Parenti. Salone Pier Lombardo. Milano (Italia). 1973. 7: Stella – Polistena.

A company of strolling players performs an AMBLET!

Une compagnie de comédiens ambulants joue un AMBLET!

288 – □ – BORIS VASSILIEV (1924): A ZORI ZDIES TIKHIJE.
1: Yourij Lioubimov. 2-3: David Boroyskij. 6: Moskovskij Teatr Dramy i Komedii na Taganke. Moskva. 1972. 7: S. Tchernov.

The elements of a military truck break apart to furnish varied spaces for the baptism by fire of a female battalion fated for extermination.

En se dissociant, les éléments d'un camion militaire fournissent les décors les plus variés pour le baptême du feu d'un bataillon féminin voué à l'extermination.

289/293

294

289/294 – △ – LUCIANO BERIO
(1925): I TRIONFI DEL PETRARCA.
2-3: Joëlle Roustan – Roger Bernard.
4: Maurice Béjart. 6: Ballet du
XXᵉ siècle. Forest-National.
Bruxelles. 1974. 7: Alain Béjart.

*Time has erased the Renown which
vanquished Death, which brought
down Chastity, which silences Love.
Phoenix, unicorn, chariots, lutes,
trumpets and laurels – all the
elements are there.*
(Claude Sarraute. Le Monde)

Le Temps a effacé la Renommée qui
a vaincu la Mort, qui a fauché la
Chasteté, qui fait taire l'Amour.
Phénix, licorne, chars, luths, trom-
pettes et lauriers, rien n'y manque.
(Claude Sarraute. Le Monde)

295/296 – □ – PETER BROOK
(1925) – **TED HUGHES :**
ORGHAST.
1: Peter Brook – Arby Ovanessian –
Geoffrey Reeves – Andreï Serban.
2-3: Eugene Lee – Franne Lee –
Jean Monod. 5: Richard Peaslee.
6: Centre International de
Recherches Théâtrales. Festival de
Shiraz. Persepolis (Iran). 1971.
7. Nicolas Tikhomiroff.

*What is the relation between verbal
and non-verbal theatre? What
happens when gesture and sound
turn into word?*

Quelle est la relation entre théâtre
verbal et théâtre non-verbal ? Que
se passe-t-il quand le geste et le son
se transforment en mot ?

297 – ☐ – ANDRE MÜLLER (1925):
DAS LETZTE PARADIES.
1: Benno Besson. 2-3: Ezio Toffolutti.
6: Volksbühne. Berlin D.D.R. 1973.
7: Harry Hirschfeld.

*The director of a zoo is persuaded
by his wife to slaughter his most
precious animals.*

Un directeur de zoo se laisse entraîner
par sa femme à abattre ses animaux
les plus précieux.

296

295

297

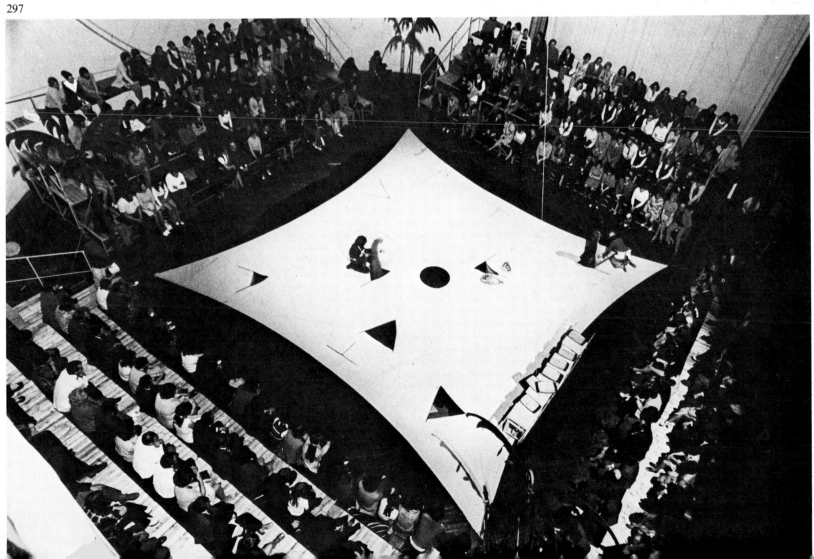

298

299

300

History – with a capital «H» – is only the pretext and alibi for the allegories that we present in an historical play.
(Patrice Chéreau)

L'Histoire – la grande – n'est que le prétexte et l'alibi des allégories que nous présentons dans un spectacle historique.
(Patrice Chéreau)

301

298/305 – □ – TANKRED DORST
(1925): TOLLER.
1: Patrice Chéreau. 2: Richard Peduzzi.
6: Théâtre National Populaire.
Villeurbanne (France). 1973.
7: Claude Bricage.

*Peduzzi's designs are decisive. The
alternation of locales – a place
where people seek to implement
certain political ideas and another
space in which the effects of those
policies are lived – is his idea, an
idea that he's pushed to an extreme,
to the level of visual hallucination,
without ever deserting the realm of
maniacal realism.*
(Patrice Chéreau)

Les décors de Peduzzi sont décisifs.
L'alternance des lieux : un lieu où
les gens essayent de mener une
politique et un second lieu où elle
est vécue, est une idée à lui – idée
que, lui, a poussée très loin, jusqu'à
l'onirisme en restant dans un
réalisme maniaque.
(Patrice Chéreau)

302

303

304

305

306 – ☐ – DARIO FO (1926):
MISTERO BUFFO.
1-2: Arturo Corso. 5: Wannes
Vandevelde. 6: Internationale Nieuwe
Scene. Koninklijke Muntschouwburg.
Brussel. 1972.

*Religion is taken as a pretext to
speak of the people and their
condition.
(Arturo Corso)*

**Le fait religieux pris comme prétexte
pour parler du peuple et de sa
condition.
(Arturo Corso)**

307 – ☐ – DARIO FO (1926):
MORTE E RESURREZIONE DI
UN PUPAZZO.
1-2-3: Dario Fo. 5: Paolo Ciarchi.
6: Collettivo Teatrale La Comune.
Teatro Circolo. Milano (Italia). 1971.
7: Agnese De Donato.

*The struggle of a «dragon» against a
«puppet». The «puppet» is, simply,
fascism. The «dragon» keeps
advancing despite the battles which
are lost : it is the working class with
its avant-garde.
(Dario Fo)*

**La lutte d'un « dragon » contre un
« pantin ». Le « pantin », c'est le
fascisme. Le « dragon » avance
toujours malgré les batailles
perdues : c'est la classe ouvrière et
son avant-garde.
(Dario Fo)**

308

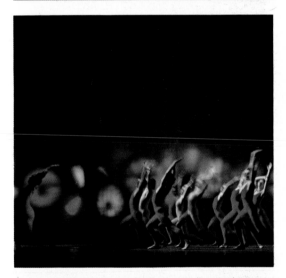

308/312 – ○ △ – PIERRE HENRY
(1927): KYLDEX 1.
1-2-3: Nicolas Schöffer.
4: Alwin Nikolais. 5: N. Schöffer –
P. Henry – A. Nikolais.
6: Hamburgische Staatsoper.
Hamburg (BRD). 1973.
7: Fritz Peyer.

*This electrical and optical ensemble
has its effects multiplied at the end
of the evening by the installation
across from the public, of a huge
triangular tunnel with mirrored
sides, which gives the spectators the
illusion of being inside a translucent
prism.*
(Claude Baignères. Had)

...Cet ensemble électrique et optique
verra en fin de soirée ses effets
multipliés à l'infini par l'installation,
face à la salle, d'un immense
tunnel triangulaire aux parois de
glace qui donnera au spectateur
l'illusion d'être installé à l'intérieur
d'un prisme translucide.
(Claude Baignères. Had)

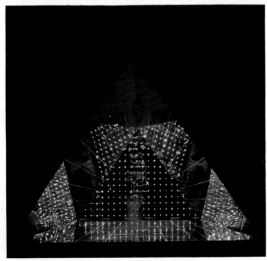

309 / 312

313/315 – ☐ – PETER HACKS
(1928): OMPHALE.
1: Ruth Berghaus. 2-3: Andreas
Reinhardt. 5: Friedrich Goldmann.
6: Berliner Ensemble. Berlin D.D.R.
1972. 7: Maria Steinfeldt.

*In the court of Omphale, Herakles,
dressed as a woman, seeks only to
live out his love : but ceasing to be
a hero will be no help in changing
the way of the world.*

A la cour d'Omphale, Hercule, en
habits de femme, veut seulement
vivre son amour : en cessant d'être
un héros, il ne réussira pas davan-
tage à changer le cours du monde.

316 – ☐ – PETER HACKS (1928):
ADAM UND EVA.
1: Dieter Stürmer.
2: Ary Oechslin. 3: Elisabeth Wittig.
6: Stadttheater. Bern. 1974.
7: Sandra Sibiglia.

*Man fully realizes himself in the
transgression of God's commandments.*

L'Homme s'accomplit dans la
transgression des interdits de Dieu.

317 – ☐ – GEZA REZVANI (1928):
CAPITAINE SCHELLE, CAPITAINE
ECÇO. 1: Jean-Pierre Vincent.
2-3: Patrice Cauchetier. 6: Théâtre de
l'Espérance. Salle Firmin Gémier.
Palais de Chaillot. Paris. 1971.
7: M. Vergnolle.

*A fable dealing with conflicts among
oil companies.*

Une fable à propos des conflits entre
compagnies pétrolières.

**318 – ☐ – ALBERTAS
LAURINCIUKAS** (1928):
VIDUTINE MOTERIS.
1: Juozas Miltinis. 2: Vitalijus Mozuras.
3: Viktorija Gatavynaité. 5: Eduardas
Balsys. 6: Dramos Teatras. Panevezys
(S.S.S.R.). 1972. 7: Eduardas Korizna.

319/323 – ☐ – PETER HACKS
(1928): MARGARETE IN AIX.
1: Benno Besson. 2-3: Helmut Brade –
Ezio Toffolutti. 5: Siegfried Matthus.
6: Volksbühne. Berlin D.D.R. 1973.

7: Harry Hirschfeld.

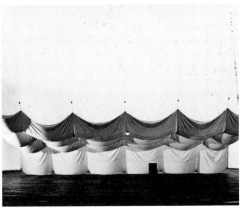

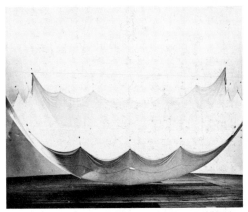

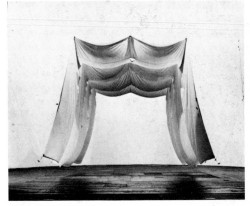

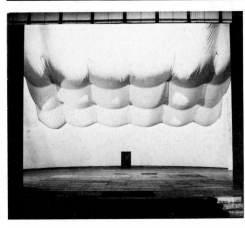

324/328 – □ – HEINER MÜLLER
(1929): ZEMENT.
1: Ruth Berghaus. 2-3: Andreas
Reinhardt. 5: Paul Dessau. 6: Berliner
Ensemble. Berlin D.D.R. 1973.
7: Maria Steinfeldt.

*During the difficult early days of the
Soviet Union, socialism begins with
the construction of a cement factory.*

**Dans les débuts difficiles de
l'U.R.S.S., le socialisme commence
avec la construction d'une usine de
ciment.**

329

329 – ○ – GALT MACDERMOT
(1930): THE TWO GENTLEMEN
OF VERONA. 1: Ebbe Langberg.
2: Tom Reimer. 3: Ellis Groenborg.
4: Noel Hickam. 5: Mel Shapiro.
6: Aalborg Teater. Aalborg (Danmark).
1972. 7: Buus Jensen.

330

330 – △ – MAKOTO MOROI
(1930): KARASU.
1: Tamehisa Endô. 2-3: Kaoru
Kanamori. 4: Yoshihisa Endô.
6: Kôseinenkin Hall. Tokyo. 1970.
7: Yoshiaki Hayashida.

331 – □ – TITUS POPOVICI
(1930): PUTEREA SI ADEVARUL.
1-2: Liviu Ciulei. 3: Doris Jurgea.
6: Teatrul Lucia Sturdza Bulandra
(Studio). Bucuresti. 1973.
7: Clara Spitzer.

331

332/333 – □ – GERHARD RÜHM
(1930): OPHELIA UND DIE
WÖRTER. 1: Jan Franksen.
2: Robert Bohrer.
6: Theater am Neumarkt. Zürich
(Helvetia). 1971. 7: Leonard Zubler.

*Ophelia's entire text by Shakespeare.
But no one answers her.*

**Tout le texte de l'Ophélie de
Shakespeare : aucun partenaire ne
lui répond.**

334 – □ – DEREK WALCOTT
(1930): IN A FINE CASTLE.
1: Derek Walcott. 2: Richard
Montgomery. 3: Sally Thompson.
6: Creative Arts Theatre.
University of the West Indies.
Kingston (Jamaica – West Indies).
1970. 7: Richard Montgomery.

332

*A decadent white French Creole
family of long-standing status in
Port of Spain, and the Black/White
syndrome against a background of
Carnival.*

**A Port d'Espagne, une vieille
famille créole française en train de
se défaire et le syndrome Blanc/
Noir sur fond de Carnaval.**

333

335/338 – △ – ALVIN AILEY (1931)
– ALICE COLTRANE –
LAURA NYRO : CRY.
4: Alvin Ailey.
6: The City Center Theatre.
New York (U.S.A.). 1971.
7: Chantal Gaulin.

339/342 – □ – ROGER PLANCHON
(1931): LE COCHON NOIR.
1: Roger Planchon. 2: Luciano Damiani.
3: Jacques Schmidt. 5: Groupe
La Bamboche. 6: Théâtre National
Populaire. Villeurbanne (France). 1974.
7: Rajak Ohanian.

*A rural community where the feudal
world meets the industrial era.*

**Une communauté villageoise à la
charnière du monde féodal et de
l'ère industrielle.**

334

335/338

339/342

343 – □ – FERNANDO ARRABAL
(1932): ILS MIRENT MÊME DES
MENOTTES AUX FLEURS.
1: Lodewijk de Boer. 2-3: Simon
Kramer. 5: Willem Breuker.
6: Toneelgroep Studio. De Brakke
Grond. Amsterdam. 1970.
7: Ad van Gessel.

344 – □ – FERNANDO ARRABAL
(1932): LE JARDIN DES DÉLICES.
1: (Jan Franksen).
2-3: Ambrosius Humm.
6: Theater am Neumarkt. Zürich
(Helvetia). 1971.
7: Leonard Zubler.

345 – □ – ARSA JOVANOVIC
(1932): DAVOLOV PECAT.
1: Arsa Jovanovic. 2: Miomir Denic.
3: Ljiljana Dragovic. 5: Baronijan
Vartkes. 6: Narodno pozoriste.
Teatar pozorisne Komune « Krug
101 ». Beograd. 1971.
7: Steva Bogdanovic.

346 – △ – MARGALIT OVED
(1932): YONAT ADEN.
2-3: David Sharir. 4: Margalit Oved.
6: Teatron Machol Shel Margalit
Oved. Israël. 1971.

The interpret changes costumes and
characters seventeen times, taking
us back to her childhood memories,
a colorful gallery of Jewish life in
Yemen.

L'interprète change 17 fois de rôle
et de costume, nous ramenant à ses
souvenirs d'enfance : une fresque
colorée de la vie juive au Yemen.

347 – □ – PETER TERSON (1932): GEORDIE'S MARCH. 1: Barrie Rutter. 2-3: Christopher Lawrence. 6: National Youth Theatre. Shaw Theatre. London. 1973. 7: Nobby Clark.

The young apprentices of a shipyard march on London.

Les jeunes apprentis d'un chantier naval marchent sur Londres.

348 – □ – ARNOLD WESKER (1932): THE OLD ONES. 1: Arnold Wesker. 2: Rudolf Heinrich. 3: Reinhard Heinrich. 6: Münchner Kammerspiele. München (BRD). 1973.

Scenes of Jewish life in a big city.

Des scènes de vie juive au cœur d'une grande ville.

347

349 – □ – E.A. WHITEHEAD (1933): THE FOURSOME. 1-2: Hannah Bjarnhof. 3: Ellis Groenborg. 6: Aalborg Teater. Koelderscenen. Aalborg (Danmark). 1972. 7: Buus Jensen.

A semi-sociological study of the courting behaviour of the young working-class male.
(Ronald Hayman)

Une étude semi-sociologique du comportement amoureux des jeunes mâles de la classe ouvrière.
(Ronald Hayman)

348

350 – □ – YAAKOV SHABTAI (1933): NAMER CHAVARBUROT. 1: Oded Kotler. 2-3: Ruth Dar. 6: Teatron Ironi Haifa. Haifa (Israël). 1974. 7: Sadeh.

351/352 – △ – KRZYSZTOF PENDERECKI (1933): TALTELA. 2-3: David Sharir. 4: Mirale Sharon. 6: Lahakat Machol Bat-Sheva. Tel-Aviv. 1974. 7: Mula-Haramaty.

An atmosphere of siege and suffocation.

Une atmosphère de siège et de suffocation.

349

350

351

352

353/354 – □ – **GHENNADIJ BOKAREV** (1934): STALIEVARY.
1: Oleg Jefremov.
2-3: Iossif Soumbatashvili.
5: Edouard Kolmanovskij.
6: Moskovskij Khoudojestvennyj Akademitcheskij Teatr imeni Gorkogo. Moskva. 1972. 7: Igor Aleksandrov.

I worked for a month in a blast-furnace.
(Oleg Jefremov)

J'ai travaillé un mois comme fondeur dans un haut-fourneau...
(Oleg Jefremov)

355/356 – ☐ – EDWARD BOND
(1935): LEAR.
1: Hans Lietzau. 2: Achim Freyer.
6: Schiller Theater. Berlin (West). 1973.
7: Ilse Buhs.

A savage indictment of authority.
All power corrupts.

Un violent réquisitoire contre
l'autorité. Tout pouvoir corrompt.

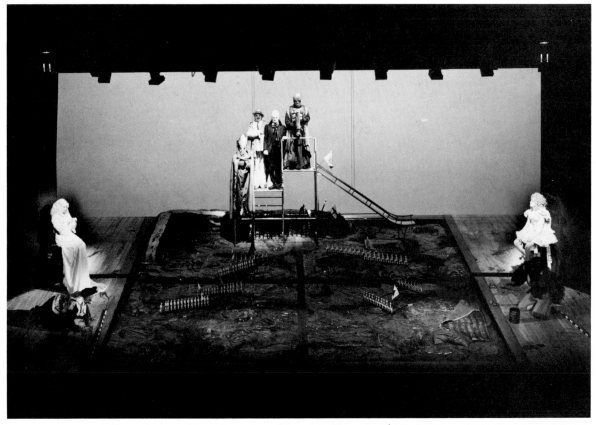

356   355

357/362 – □ – HISASHI INOUE
(1935): YABUHARA KENGYO.
1: Koichi Kimura. 2-3: Setsu Asakura.
5: Shigéru Inoué. 6: Gogatsu-sha.
Seibu Gekijô. Tokyo. 1973.
7: Shigéko Higuchi.

*The story of a blind man about
200 years ago. Most of the characters
are blind.*

L'histoire d'un aveugle voici
environ 200 ans. La plupart des
personnages sont aveugles.

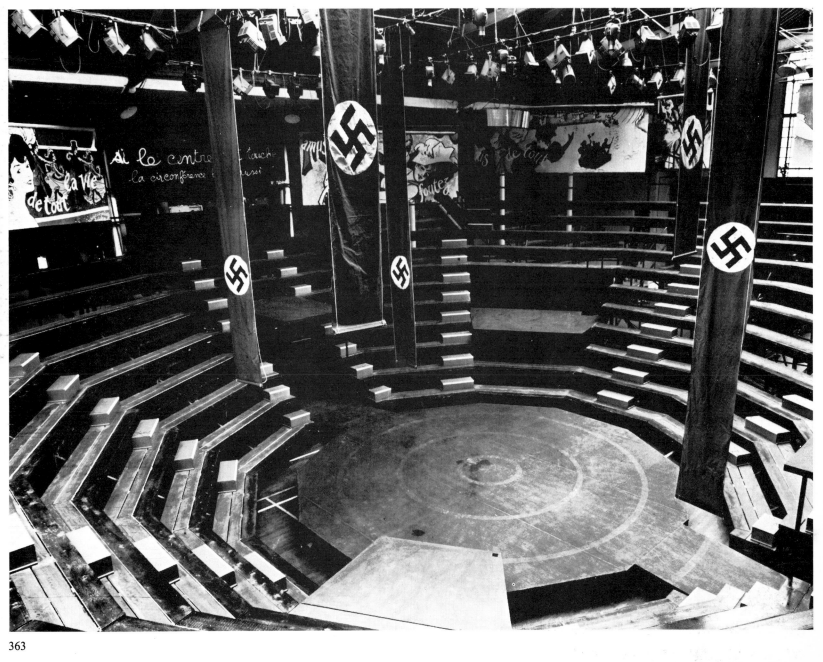

363

363 – □ – CHRISTIAN LIGER
(1935): CHRONIQUE DE LA VIE
ET DE LA MORT D'HITLER.
1 : Jo Tréhard. 2-3 : Jo Tréhard –
A. Chevalier. 5 : Armand Bex.
6 : Comédie de Caen. Stade de Caen
(France). 1971.

365

364/366 – □ – ROCHELLE OWENS
(1936) : FUTZ.
1 : Alan Robb. 2-3 : Richard Montgomery.
6 : Creative Arts Centre. University of
the West Indies (Jamaica – West Indies).
1970.

364   366

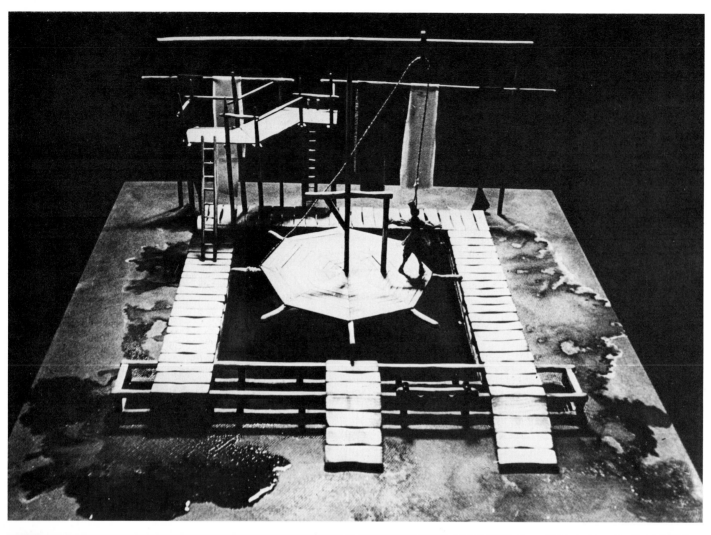

367 – □ – ARIS GHEJKINE (1936):
LEGHENDA O KAUPO.
1: Olghert Kroder.
2-3: Andris Freiberg.
6: Dramatitcheskij Teatr imeni
Leona Pegla. Valmiera (S.S.S.R.). 1973.
7: Yourij Ikonnikov.

*The baptism of the baltic tribes by
teutonic warriors in the year 1210,
and the treason of their chief Kaupe.*

Le baptême des tribus baltes par les
chevaliers teutoniques en 1210 et
la trahison du chef Kaupe.

**368 – □ – EDOUARD
RADZINSKIJ** (1936):
MONOLOG O BRAKIE.
1: Kama Ghinkas.
2-3: Edouard Kotcherghine.
5: Valerij Sevastjanov.
6: Leningradskij Akademitcheskij
Teatr Komedii. Leningrad (S.S.S.R.).
1973.

The fallings out of a young family.

Les brouilles d'un jeune ménage.

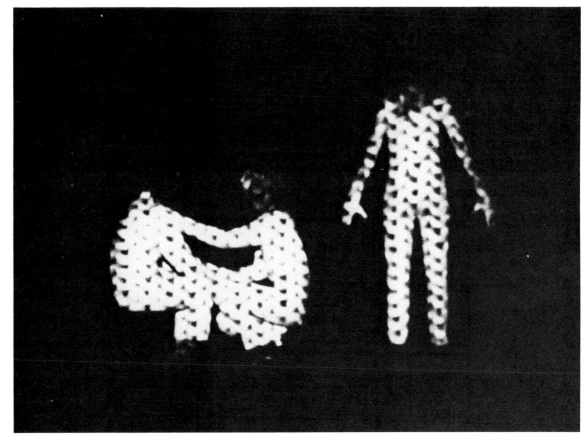

369 – □ – ADRI BOON (1937) –
JAN VAN AS – LUCEBERT :
FATA BANANA.
1: Adri Boon. 2-3: Studio Scarabee.
5: Otto Ketting.
6: Studio Scarabee. Den Haag
(Nederland) 1971. 7: Rob van Loon.

*The actors don't play roles; they
«function» as liaison agents in a
collage of images, movements, text
and music.*

Les acteurs n'interprètent pas un
rôle : ils « fonctionnent » comme
agents de liaison au sein d'un collage d'images, de mouvements, de
texte et de musique.

**370/373 – □ – LODEWIJK DE
BOER** (1937): ZEVEN MANIEREN
OM EEN RIVIER OVER TE
STEKEN. 1: Albert-André Lheureux.
2-3: Jean-Marie Fievez. 5: Daniel
Dejean. 6: Théâtre de l'Esprit Frap-
peur. Bruxelles. 1973. 7: Jean-Marie
Fievez (370/372) – Nicolas Treatt (373).

*Different stories unfold at different
times without beginning or end.
(Lodewijk de Boer)*

Différentes histoires se déroulent
à des époques différentes sans
commencement ni fin.
(Lodewijk de Boer)

374/375 – ☐ – COPI (1937 ?) –
JÉRÔME SAVARY : GOOD BYE
MISTER FREUD. 1: Jérôme Savary.
2: Michel Lebois – Patrick Chauveau.
4: Victor Upshaw. 5: J. Coutureau –
J. Savary – M. Yonnet – E. Rondo –
M. Lima – J.Cl. D'Agostini.
6: Grand Magic Circus – Festival
d'Automne. Théâtre de la Porte
Saint-Martin. Paris. 1974.
7: Chantal Gaulin.

*An Opéra-Tango written by Copi
and Jérôme Savary, with Freud,
Mimi Freud and Dracula, the red
Countess, Al Capone, Shakespeare,
Gustave the Bear, and the King of
the Mongols...*

**Un Opéra-Tango écrit par Copi et
Jérôme Savary, avec Freud, Mimi
Freud et Dracula, la Comtesse Rouge,
Al Capone, Shakespeare, l'ours
Gustave et le roi des Mongols...**

376

377

376/377 – ☐ – GERBEN
HELLINGA (1937):
KEES DE JONGEN.
1: Peter Oosthoek.
2-3: Roger Chailloux – Peter Oosthoek.
6: Toneelgroep Centrum.
Stadsschouwburg. Haarlem
(Nederland). 1970. 7: F. Lemaire.

*Caught between childhood fantasies
and hard realities, Kees breaks into
a K1 and K2.*

**Ballotté entre les fantaisies de l'en-
fance et la dure réalité, Kees se
dédouble en K 1 et K 2.**

378

378 – ☐ – TOM STOPPARD
(1937): JUMPERS. 1: Horst Balzer.
2-3: Fritz Butz. 4: Waslaw Orlikowsky.
5: Cedric Dumont.
6: Schauspielhaus. Zürich (Helvetia).
1974. 7: Leonard Zubler.

*A desperate farce about the inability
of man to live with his own
rationalism.*

**Une farce désespérée sur l'incapacité
de l'homme à vivre son propre
rationalisme.**

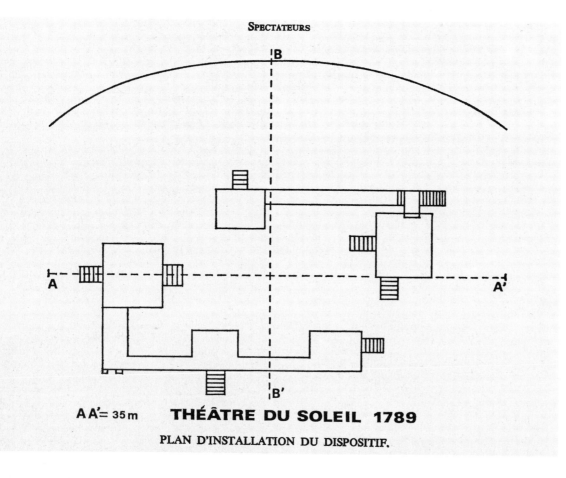

B

A ----------------------------------- A'

B'

AA'= 35 m   **THÉÂTRE DU SOLEIL 1789**
PLAN D'INSTALLATION DU DISPOSITIF.

381

382

**379/384 – □ – ARIANE
MNOUCHKINE** (1939) – **LE
THÉÂTRE DU SOLEIL :** 1789
(LA RÉVOLUTION DOIT
S'ARRÊTER A LA PERFECTION
DU BONHEUR).
1 : (Ariane Mnouchkine).
2 : Roberto Moscoso.
3 : Françoise Tournafond –
Christiane Candries.
6 : Théâtre du Soleil. La Cartoucherie.
Vincennes (France). 1970.
7 : M. Vergnolle (380/382/383) –
Michel Berger (381/384).

The actors of the Théâtre du Soleil
play *the comic performers, the
mountebanks, the jugglers of the fair,
and it is they who* play *the characters,
great or small, of 1789. They play
them, to be specific, from the popular
point of view, as the people might
imagine, feel, live and suffer the
revolution.*
(Arturo Lazzari)

Les acteurs du Théâtre du Soleil
jouent **les acteurs comiques, les
saltimbanques, les jongleurs de la
foire, et ce sont ces derniers qui**
jouent **les personnages, grands ou
humbles, de 1789.** Ils les jouent,
précisément, du point de vue populaire; comme le peuple put imagi-
ner, ressentir, vivre et souffrir la
révolution.
(Arturo Lazzari)

383

384

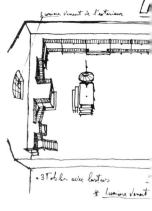

386

385

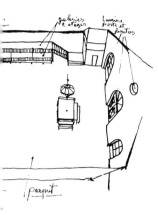

387

388

389

**385/390 – □ – ARIANE
MNOUCHKINE** (1939) –
LE THÉÂTRE DU SOLEIL : 1793
(LA CITÉ RÉVOLUTIONNAIRE
EST DE CE MONDE).
1 : (Ariane Mnouchkine).
2 : B. Bauchau – J.N. Cordier –
A. Ferreira – Cl. Forget –
G. Cl. François – L. de Grandmaison –
R. Moscoso – A. Salomon.
3 : J. Cl. Barriera – N. Ferreira –
Ch. Forget – F. Tournafond.
6 : Théâtre du Soleil. La Cartoucherie.
Vincennes (France). 1972.
7 : M. Vergnolle (386/388/390) –
Michel Berger (385).

*In 1793 the actors of the Théâtre du
Soleil no longer play the carnival folk
who act out stories of the Revolution,
rather they play the role of the
sans-culottes who recall the
Revolution for themselves.
(Ariane Mnouchkine)*

**Dans 1793, ce seront non plus les
acteurs du Théâtre du Soleil qui
jouent le rôle de bateleurs qui
racontent la Révolution, mais les
acteurs qui joueront le rôle de
sectionnaires, de sans-culottes qui
se racontent la Révolution.
(Ariane Mnouchkine)**

390

391

394

391/393 – □ – FREDERIC BAAL
(1940): I. 1: Anne West.
2-3: Olivier Strebelle.6: Théâtre
Laboratoire Vicinal. Bruxelles. 1974.
7: Thierry Jonard.

*There is no story, just a succession of
scenes which could be played in any
order.*
(Frédéric Baal)

Il n'y a pas d'histoire, mais une suite
de scènes jouables à la limite dans
n'importe quel ordre.
(Frédéric Baal)

394 – □ – PETER HANDKE (1942):
DAS MÜNDEL WILL VORMUND
SEIN. 1: Hans Peter Fitzi.
2: Jochen Luft. 3: Ricarda Toppy-
Dressier. 6: Forumtheater. Berlin.
(West). 1970. 7: Harry Croner.

395 – □ – PETER HANDKE (1942):
DER RITT ÜBER DEN BODENSEE.
1: Claude Régy. 2-3: Ezio Frigerio.
6: Espace Cardin. Paris. 1974.
7: Michel Berger.

*Rather than «characters», they are,
at least in the beginning, two-
dimensional images, empty images.
Then they become what they say,
they fill themselves with memories.*
(Peter Handke)

Plutôt que des « personnages », ce
sont, en tout cas au début du spectacle, des images en deux dimen-
sions, des images vides. Et puis ils
deviennent ce qu'ils disent, ils se
remplissent de souvenirs.
(Peter Handke)

396 – □ – PETER HANDKE
(1942): DER RITT ÜBER DEN
BODENSEE. 1: Horst Zankl.
2-3: Ambrosius Humm.
6: Theater am Neumarkt. Zürich
(Helvetia). 1972. 7: Leonard Zubler.

395

396

399

397

398

397/404 – □ – **JÉRÔME SAVARY**
(1942) – **GRAND MAGIC CIRCUS :**
DE MOÏSE A MAO.
1: Jérôme Savary. 2: M. Lebois –
P. Chauveau – Ch. Marty – Sabine.
3: Michel Dussarat – Michel Debats.
5: J. Coutureau – M. Yonnet –
J. Savary. 6: Grand Magic Circus.
Théâtre National de Strasbourg.
Strasbourg (France). 1973.
7: Cl. Nougier (397/404) –
Ch. Weiss (398) – S. Strosser (403) –
G. Messora (399) – J. Prayer (402).

400

401

Mankind's epic, its history, its stories : a succession of failed loves and victorious wars, as suggested by the troupe of Vienna's Follies, stuck in Nevada while awaiting a subsidy from Queen Victoria who is content to send a birthday cake. (Colette Godard)

403

404

L'épopée de l'homme, son histoire, ses histoires : une suite d'amours ratées et de guerres réussies, représentée par la troupe des Vienna's Follies, bloquée dans le Nevada en attendant une subvention de la reine Victoria qui se contente d'envoyer un gâteau d'anniversaire. (Colette Godard)

402

405

406

405 – □○ – ROBERT WILSON (1943) – **ALAN LLOYD :** A LETTER FOR QUEEN VICTORIA. 1: Robert Wilson. 2-3: Fred Kolouch. 4: Andrew de Groat. 6: Festival de la Rochelle – Festival d'Automne. Théâtre des Variétés. Paris .1974. 7: M. Vergnolle.

The world of torturing beauty.

Le monde de la beauté torturante.

406 – □ – RAINER WERNER FASSBINDER (1946): BREMER FREIHEIT. 1: Rainer Werner Fassbinder. 2: Wilfried Minks. 3: Wilfried Minks – Maja Lemcke. 6: Theater der Freien Hansestadt. Concordia. Bremen (BRD). 1972. 7: Ilse Buhs.

The oppression of women in a masculine world.
Geesche Gottfried, given over to judicial punishment on April 21, 1831, after poisoning her parents, brother, fiancé, two husbands, her three children, and five other people.

L'oppression de la femme dans le monde masculin.
Geesche Gottfried, livrée au supplice le 21 avril 1831, après avoir empoisonné ses parents, son frère, son fiancé, deux maris, ses trois enfants et cinq autres personnes.

407 – □ – CHRISTOPHER HAMPTON (1946): TOTAL ECLIPSE. 1: Adrian Brine. 2-3: Jean-Marie Fievez. 6: Théâtre du Rideau de Bruxelles. Palais des Beaux Arts. Bruxelles. 1973.

Verlaine and Rimbaud... the artist and society...

Verlaine et Rimbaud... L'artiste et la société...

407

408 – □ – FRANZ XAVER KROETZ (1946): STALLERHOF. 1-2: Ulrich Heising – Karl Kneidl. 6: Deutsches Schauspielhaus in Hamburg. Berliner Theatertreffen. Berlin (West). 1973. 7: Ilse Buhs.

A 58 year old farm worker impregnates the farmer's daughter (18), a retarded girl : the farmer kills the worker's dearest friend, his dog.

Un ouvrier agricole (58 ans), engrosse la fille du fermier (18 ans), une faible d'esprit. Le fermier tue ce que l'ouvrier avait de plus cher au monde, son chien.

408

409

410

409/421 – ◯ – ANDREW LLOYD WEBBER (1948): JESUS CHRIST SUPERSTAR.
1: Keita Asari. 2-3: Kaoru Kanamori.
4: Takashi Yamada. 5: Timothy Rice.
6: Gékidan-Shiki. Nakano Sun Plaza Hall. Tokyo. 1973.
7: Shigéko Higuchi – Jinkichi Sekiguchi.

411

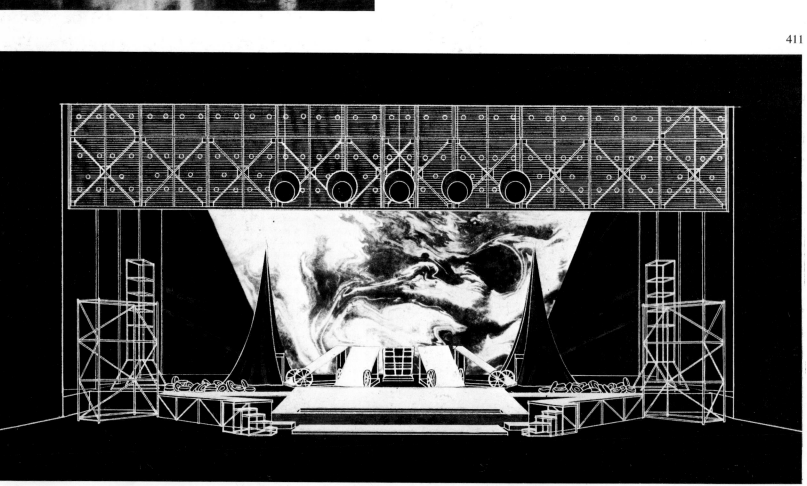

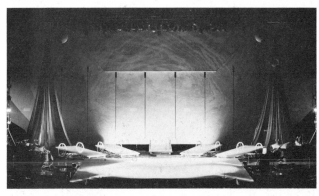

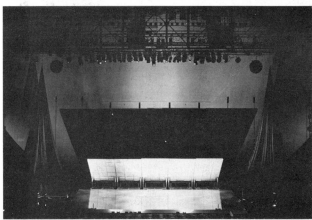

412

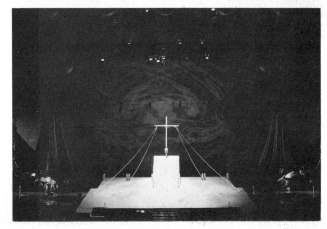

418

419

420

421

INDEX OF ILLUSTRATIONS LISTED UNDER DIRECTORS, CHOREOGRAPHERS, DESIGNERS AND COSTUME DESIGNERS

BIBLIOGRAPHICAL REFERENCES

In the preparation of this book we consulted a great variety of recent publications concerning the theatre. We should like to include in our expressions of gratitude, their authors, editors and publishers.

First of all, the many books. For example, for scenography: Denis Bablet, *Svoboda* (Lausanne: L'Age d'homme, 1970); Jarka Burian, *The Scenography of Josef Svoboda* (Middletown: Wesleyan University Press, 1971); Jacques Polieri, *Scénographie. Sémiographie* (Paris: Denoël/Gonthier, 1971); *Stage Design throughout the World since 1960* (London: Harrap; New-York: Theatre Arts Books - 1973); *Scenographia hungarica* (Budapest: Corvina Kiado, 1973); Howard Bay, *Stage Design* (New York: Drama Book Specialists/Publishers, 1974). And, treatises such as: H. Burris-Meyer and E.C. Cole, *Scenery for the Theatre* (Boston: Little, Brown, and Co., 1972); S. Selden and T. Rezzuto, *Essentials of Stage Scenery* (New York: Appleton, Century, Crofts, 1972); H.C. Heffner, S. Selden, H.D. Sellman, and F.P. Walkup, *Modern Theatre Practice* (New York: Appleton, Century, Crofts, 1973); Bruno Mello, *Trattato di scenotecnica* (Milano: Görlich, 1973). See also various catalogues like: *Prague Quadriennal of Theatre Design and Architecture* (Praha: Divadelni Ustav, 1971) or *Contemporary Stage Design U.S.A.* (New York: International Theatre Institute of the United States, 1974).

For architectural matters: *Les Lieux du spectacle – Osaka 70* (Boulogne-sur-Seine: L'Architecture d'Aujourd'hui, 1970); Hannelore Schubert, *Moderner Theaterbau* (Stuttgart-Bern: Karl Krämer, 1971); Roberto Aloi, *Teatri e auditori* (Milano: Hoepli, 1972).

For lighting: Richard Pilbrow, *Stage Lighting* (London: Studio Vista, 1970); Emmet W. Bongar, *Practical Stage Lighting* (New York: Rosen, 1971).

On contemporary authors: M. Anderson, J. Guicharnaud, and others, *Crowell's Handbook of Contemporary Drama* (New York: Thomas Y. Crowell, 1971); Sylviane Bonnerot, *Visages du théâtre contemporain* (Paris: Masson, 1971); James Vinson, editor, *Contemporary Dramatists* (London: St. James Press; New York: St. Martin's Press – 1973); *25 ans de décentralisation: les spectacles* (Paris: ATAC informations, 1973).

On recent tendencies and movements: Hans Hoppe, *Das Theater der Gegenstände* (Bensberg-Frankenforst: Basilius Presse-Schäuble Verlag, 1971); John Percival, *Experimental Dance* (New York: Universe Books, 1971); K.M. Taylor, *People's Theatre in Amerika* (New York: Drama Book Specialists/Publishers, 1972); *Le Théâtre dans le Monde. World Theatre* (Varsovie: Polish Centre of the I.T.I., 1972); James Roose-Evans, *Experimental Theatre from Stanislavski to Today* (London: Studio Vista, 1973); *Théâtre et contemporanéité* (Bucarest; Revue Roumaine, 1973); John Weisman, *Guerilla Theatre. Scenarios for Revolution* (New York: Anchor, 1973).

On sociological aspects: Emile Copfermann, *La Mise en crise théâtrale* (Paris: Maspero, 1972); Michèle Vessillier, *La Crise du théâtre privé* (Paris: Presses Universitaires de France, 1973).

Occasionally an entire work is devoted to a single company: Joseph Chaikin, *The Presence of the Actor: Notes on The Open Theatre* (New York: Atheneum, 1972). Or to a single director: Franco Quadri, *Il Rito perduto. Luca Ronconi* (Torino: G. Einaudi, 1973). Or to a single production: *Théâtre du Soleil, 1789* (Paris: Stock, 1971); A.C.H. Smith, *Orghast at Persepolis* (New York: Viking, 1972); *Théâtre du Soleil, 1793* (Paris: Stock, 1972); E. Nassour and R. Broderick, *Rock Opera: The Creation of Jesus Christ Superstar* (New York: Hawthorn Books, 1973); L. Zonneveld, *Toneelwerkgroep Proloog "Neus & Ko"* (Amsterdam: Van Gennep, 1974).

We have also looked at certain remarkable programs: by the Schaubühne for *Das Sparschwein* and *Peer Gynt* (Berlin: Albert Hentrich, 1971 and 1973); by the Théâtre du Parvis for *Mesure pour mesure* (Bruxelles: Le Théâtre, 1972); by the Centre International de Créations Théâtrales for *Timon d'Athènes* in a French adaptation by Jean-Claude Carrière (Paris: the Center, 1974).

And we should not leave out the various annual publications: *Israel Theatre, Jahressonderheft "Theater Heute", Nederlands Theater Jaarboek, The American Theatre, Theatre in Denmark, Theatre Review*, etc. Finally, the periodicals: *ATAC Informations, Bühnentechnische Rundschau, Drama, Interscena, L'Avant-Scène, Theatre in Poland, Les Cahiers Théâtre Louvain, Nouvelles du théâtre finlandais, Opernwelt, Plays and Players, Sipario, The Drama Review, Theater der Zeit, Theater Heute, Theatre Design and Technology, Théâtre et Université, Travail Théâtral*, etc

CONTENTS